P9-DVO-820

Praise for *Darn Easy* and Peggy McColl and Brian Proctor

In *Darn Easy*, Brian and Peggy have done a wonderful job of conveying their success-generating steps for you to follow. Like master astronomers charting the stars, they have charted the various ideas that they have used to make life darn easy for them. Pick a target and follow their directions. You'll be amazed and delighted by the results.

—From the Foreword by Bob Proctor, teacher of "The Secret," bestselling author of *You Were Born Rich,* and chairman and cofounder of the Proctor Gallagher Institute

Whether you're a seasoned businessperson or an entrepreneur just starting out, *Darn Easy* offers life-changing strategies and useful tips to lead you to greater ease, a larger sense of purpose, and more joy and prosperity in your business.

—Joy van Hemert, CEO of Green Earth Properties, LLC

Peggy McColl and Brian Proctor have created a fantastic, inspiring guide that shows entrepreneurs how to set clear goals and amplify success while working less and fully enjoying life. *Darn Easy* is a must-read.

—Kristi Ling, author of *Operation Happiness*

The magnificence of learning how to do anything easily is explained simply in this easy-to-read, easy-to-apply blueprint for living. Peggy and Brian offer us the latest strategies to being successful in business and in life. Finally, a simple approach to living life with joy, grace, and ease!

—Julie Jones Hamilton, coauthor of *The Change 4: Insights into Self-Empowerment*

Darn Easy is chock-full of incredible, life-enhancing, actionable information designed to provide you with clear insights and strategies that will lead to awesome abundance with ease! Peggy McColl and Brian Proctor are the real deal. Not only do they advise to be "100 percent committed to your own growth," their collective wisdom shared throughout this book is based on timeless and priceless principles that work! The sample visualization transcript could be worth millions on their own, when put into practice. Study *Darn Easy* and keep reviewing it for the next 90 days! You will find your life aimed directly at Growth, Prosperity, and Success!

—Bruce McGregor, author of *GPS Wealth*

Setting clear goals and being in the right state of mind to bring them to fruition is one of life's biggest challenges. But doing it easily? In *Darn Easy*, Peggy McColl and Brian Proctor have presented a foolproof way to achieve your objectives with ease. Follow their recommendations and you'll be living the life of your dreams in record time.

—Mick Petersen, author of *Stella and the Timekeepers*

Wow! I loved it! Everything you need in one book to live to your fullest potential! Peggy and Brian have truly created a positive vehicle for a successful life that you drive in any direction you want to go. They have given us the map and keys to our own success! Open the door, turn it on, and get ready to drive in the fast lane! Thank you for making the achievement of my dreams so darn easy!

—Leanne Sexton, founder of Touch a Heart Networks
and author of *The Book of Knowings*

I have the privilege of knowing Brian personally and professionally, and he's the real deal. Brian was born and raised in the laws of attraction, and I watch Brian have fun and make money effortlessly every day, while doing the things he loves with the people he loves. If he's giving guidance, I recommend listening. This could be the one book that will change your life.

—Wendy Newman, MA, founder and executive
producer of Innertaining™ Media

Want to lead a successful life with ease, while having fun? Read *Darn Easy*. I've known Peggy for the past 20 years, and she has made it darn easy for thousands of people. Why not you?

—Bob Urichuck, author of *Velocity Selling*

This book features an abundance of great tips and exercises for increasing profit and decreasing stress, as well as creating habits that will help make success easy. *Darn Easy* is a must-read!

—Judy O'Beirn, creator and coauthor of the
Unwavering Strength book series

Darn Easy is a magnificent tool kit of vital life principles and practices that will, if used, help you easily create an extraordinary life of wealth and abundance. Peggy and Brian share from their hearts with authenticity, wisdom, real-life success, and a burning desire for everyone to live in abundance. The content is powerful, useble, and life-transforming. This book is included in my Wisdom Library, to be studied and referred to often.

—Jo Campbell Hipkin, ICF Professional Certified Coach

Darn Easy has a unique twist on goal achievement and the entrepreneurial mindset that is seriously needed. It is so relevant in today's world of fast change and information overload. Peggy and Brian provide rich expertise, not just on creating the life or business that you desire but, more important, they dive deeply into the intrinsic work that is missed by so many business books. The easy-to-follow practical applications are unique and worth gold! I highly recommend this book.

—Karen Smith, founder of findingpurpose.com

Here are gems of practical wisdom. Act on Peggy and Brian's advice and you *will* advance in the direction of your dream. It's that simple! They know what it takes to be successful—online and beyond. What's more, they are heart-centered teachers. They truly walk the talk and delight in giving you the tools to shine in the work you love!

—Robin Blackburn McBride
transformational life coach and speaker

Peggy is a champion at introducing wake-up calls to take charge of your life. The awesome strategies and pragmatic advice in *Darn Easy*, when embraced, will inspire you to lead an extraordinary and maximized life—right now.

—May Barnes, life coach and speaker

DARN
EASY

DARN EASY

WORK HALF AS HARD,
EARN TWICE AS MUCH,
WHILE LIVING THE LIFE
OF YOUR DREAMS

PEGGY McCOLL and **BRIAN PROCTOR**

New York Chicago San Francisco Athens London Madrid
Mexico City Milan New Delhi Singapore Sydney Toronto

1 2 3 4 5 6 7 8 9 0   DOC/DOC   1 2 1 0 9 8 7 6 5

ISBN   978-1-259-58293-6
MHID   1-259-58293-0

e-ISBN   978-1-259-58294-3
e-MHID   1-259-58294-9

Library of Congress Cataloging-in-Publication Data

Names: McColl, Peggy. | Proctor, Brian.
Title: Darn easy : work half as hard, earn twice as much, while living the
   life of your dreams / by Peggy McColl and Brian Proctor.
Description: New York : McGraw-Hill Education, 2015.
Identifiers: LCCN 2015031168| ISBN 9781259582936 (hardback) |
   ISBN 1259582930
Subjects: LCSH: Goal (Psychology) | Self-actualization (Psychology) |
   Success. | BISAC: BUSINESS & ECONOMICS / Motivational.
Classification: LCC BF505.G6 M32 2015 | DDC 650.1—dc23 LC record
available at http://lccn.loc.gov/2015031168

McGraw-Hill Education books are available at special quantity discounts to use as premiums and sales promotions or for use in corporate training programs. To contact a representative, please visit the Contact Us pages at www.mhprofessional.com.

To Bob Proctor

Contents

Foreword

Most of us grow up with the idea that if you work hard, you'll do well in life. But you probably know by now that's not true. Many who have worked hard all their lives have never really made it happen.

The ideas you'll find in this book aren't anything like the ones most of us grew up with. Yet strange and marvelous things will begin to happen as you start to incorporate them into your life.

I've known Peggy McColl for the last 35 years, and I have known Brian all of his life. Brian is my son, and I'm very proud of his accomplishments. I'm proud of Peggy's accomplishments as well.

When they told me they were teaming up to write this book, I knew that it would be a great book because they both practice what you are about to read. In other words, both of them have earned a tremendous amount of money—and continue to do so. And neither one of them works hard.

Before Brian was born, I was fortunate enough to have Napoleon Hill's book *Think and Grow Rich* put in my hands. I'd like to share one part of the book that really jumped out at me.

Hill said, "If you're one of those who believe that hard work and honesty, alone, will bring riches, perish the thought! It's not true! Riches, when they come in huge quantities, are never the result of hard work! Riches come, if they come at all, in response to definite demands, based on the application of definite principles, and not by chance or luck."

Peggy and Brian have woven the essence of that principle into each page of this book. The key ingredient is what Hill said about riches coming in response to definite demands. You must demand it of yourself. This book will help you accomplish that.

I still read *Think and Grow Rich* every day because the ideas are sound. The ideas in this book are sound, too. Brian and Peggy have done a wonderful job of conveying their success-generating steps for you to follow. Like master astronomers charting the stars, they have charted the various ideas they have used to make life darn easy for them. So don't treat this book lightly. Do exactly what Peggy and Brian suggest. Pick a target and follow their directions. You'll be amazed at and delighted with the results.

Before jumping in, remember this: no amount of reading or memorizing is going to change anything in your life. It's acting on the ideas in each chapter that will produce the results you want.

Before you begin, write your goal on a card and put it in front of you. Then, as you start reading, look for ideas you can act on to reach your goal in the shortest time with the least amount of energy. And whatever you do, make sure you make it darn easy!

—Bob Proctor

Acknowledgments

We feel extremely grateful to be represented by the best literary agent in the world, Bill Gladstone. Bill is a tremendous support. Bill kindly connected us with the talented ghostwriter Randall Fitzgerald, who delivered a fabulous piece of work on time and perfectly written. We are also grateful for the warm welcome we received from the good folks at McGraw-Hill and how embraced we felt being a part of the McGraw-Hill family.

From PM: It was an easy decision to dedicate this book to the wonderful Bob Proctor, who has had such a powerful and positive influence on our lives. Bob Proctor came into my life more than three decades ago and continues to enrich, inspire, and challenge me to be more, give more, learn more, share more, and, as a result, experience more. People often ask me, "Who has had the greatest influence or impact on your life?" and I answer, "That's easy! My son, Michel; my husband, Denis; and my mentor and friend, Bob Proctor."

My son, Michel, and my grandson, James, inspire me to be a better role model to them and to the world. My husband, Denis, is my constant companion who shares everything in my life and my business and supports me in every way imaginable. My life is enriched by the men with whom I gratefully share my life.

My sister, Judy, continues to support me, my business, and my books with her unwavering strength. You are much more than a sister. You are a valued friend.

From BP: Everyone always asks me what it's like to have Bob Proctor as a father. I always smile and tell them how lucky I am. I also let them know that he is everything and more than what they ever see at a seminar, event, or interview.

Dad, you have shown me by example how to step out and really bet on myself. You have also shown me how to see adversity as just a place in time and to keep looking forward and accept it for what it is.

I have a lot to be grateful for in my life, but I can clearly say that I am most grateful to have you as my father. I could never express in words what it means to be given such unconditional support and encouragement. What I love is that you have always been that way with me as far back as I can remember. There have been many occasions throughout my life when the words you spoke to me have stuck forever.

I know that I am the person I am today because of you. I often hear your voice as I am speaking with Danny and Leanne, sharing with them wisdom that you had previously shared with me.

You have made me always want to be a better person and to constantly improve my life. This book is a direct result of your influence on me.

Introduction

Do Something Today Your Future Self Will Thank You For

We have a simple formula to offer you. It will enable you to work half as hard and profit twice as much whether your business is new or old, online or offline. It's a proven formula to make what you do for a living both fun and easy as you increase profit and decrease stress.

We both run independent businesses. We are entrepreneurs who have created very successful ventures from the comfort of our homes. We did it with ease, and we had fun doing it.

We've seen other people struggle financially, and we see people who continue to struggle. If you fall into that category, if stress is your constant companion and success remains elusive, this book is definitely for you.

When I, Peggy McColl, decided to incorporate a company in 1994, my son was two years old and I was going through a divorce, and so I had a lot to manage in my life. I had worked in the corporate world for many years and had done well at it. As I took the steps to incorporate my own business, many well-meaning people offered me unsolicited advice. Usually they cautioned me, "Don't you know that most businesses fail within the first seven years?"

"But I'm going to choose to succeed," I always responded. Failure wasn't an option. It wasn't in my vocabulary. I'm very happy to say that I'm now celebrating my twentieth year of being successful and profitable with continuous annual growth.

Brian and I decided it was time to write a book to address how you can bring more ease and fun and joy into your life while building a company and making lots of money. It's really important for a business and for your success to create the circumstances that enable you to have fun with what you do. With that enjoyment comes the feeling that everything is happening with the greatest of ease.

I learned an enduring lesson from a wonderful friend and mentor, Gay Hendricks, author of *The Big Leap*, when he asked, "Are you willing to have your life be easy some of the time?" I remember him asking me that question. Of course, I said yes. He replied, "Okay, are you willing to have your life be easy most of the time?" I remember thinking, "Is this a rhetorical question? A trick question? Is there something else coming? If I say yes, is that the wrong answer?"

Although I was slightly suspicious at the time, I answered, "Yes, I am willing to have my life be easy most of the time." He followed that up with "Are you willing to have your life be easy all the time?" When he asked me that, I felt a lot of resistance well up. I didn't know where that resistance was coming from. I didn't know if I was willing to have my life be easy all the time. Maybe you can relate to that from your own encounters with resistance.

In that moment, I thought to myself, "Is it even possible to experience life that way?" He was looking for an affirmative answer, but I had to find it within myself. I thought about it for a minute, and unlike with the first two questions, I didn't answer quickly. After a long silence, I said, "Yes, I am."

"Great!" he responded. "It *is* possible. I'm here to tell you it's possible to have your life be easy all the time."

You know what? He was right.

In this book, we talk about developing ease with money, with business, with relationships, with every part of your life. You can share this with your children, your spouse, your business partner, and your clients. It's such a little thing, yet it can make a tremendous difference. In this book, we will show you how it's done.

You Can Choose to Make Money with Ease

Every business needs to make money. If you're not making money, you'll be out of business within a short time. Yet making money isn't the only thing that's important. Your financial income needs to be supplemented with your emotional income to sustain your vision for what is possible to achieve.

Some of you may have been in the pursuit of personal development for many years. You may have read self-help books, attended consciousness workshops, or been in success training programs. Many others may find it a fairly new concept to think that cultivating personal development skills can be a key to the success of their business ventures. We will show you how evolving personally as your business evolves can ensure the long-term success of your venture while bestowing on you many blessings in your personal relationships and your overall feelings of happiness and contentment with life.

Having fun and feeling ease in your work is really a choice. You have an opportunity every day to make a new decision about what you will focus on so that your life is guided more smoothly toward success. What we show you in *Darn Easy* is how the secret of change is to focus all your energy not on fighting the old but on building the new.

The one thing that Brian's father, Bob Proctor, always impressed upon us is that everything we do, everything we experience, and every way we react is a choice. It really is a choice. When you're going through anything, step back for a moment and ask, "What am I choosing here? Am I choosing difficult and chaotic, or am I choosing ease?" Every time you step back and choose to be at ease, it flows, and it becomes habit-forming.

The whole idea that creating more success in your life is going to be painful is just a fear, a toxic thought, a choice you've made to buy into the negative. It's something that you made up, and it really doesn't have to be that way. You can choose to change your attitude about how hard achieving success will be. You can choose to make it easy. We will show you how.

There is only one person who is creating chaos in your life right now. That person stares back at you when you look in the mirror. You need to decide if you want to continue down this road of difficulty, chaos, anxiety, and failure or if you will stop and take a breath and choose to focus on having this be an enjoyable day. Ask yourself, "What can I do in this moment that can shift so that I have greater enjoyment of my business and my source of income?"

Your words are powerful engines for growth and change. They are energy in motion. If you say that you're sick and tired, chances are that you'll become sick and tired. If you say it's going to be hard, chances are that it will become hard. Maybe not always, but it's the energy in what you speak that helps determine outcomes. We're going to invite you as an exercise going forward to pay attention to your language and the impact your words have.

Everyone faces challenges. There isn't a person on this planet who doesn't face a challenge of some kind. Business owners often face more than their fair share of challenges. We'll be talking about specific ways that you can get through these challenges with the greatest of ease so that you roll with the punches and come out on top.

You Hold Your Future in Your Hands

Someone once asked Bob Proctor, "What's the greatest lesson you've ever learned about money?" He instantly knew the answer and replied, "How easy it is to make it."

How many people really believe that it's easy to make money? A lot of people think it's difficult, but it just requires a shift in your thinking.

Bob also teaches that you see yourself either in abundance or mired in debt. We are here to tell you that you'll attract whatever it is you choose to see. Brian and I aren't going to say that we see ourselves in abundance 100 percent of the time, but we know for a fact that we each focus on that the majority of the time.

It all comes down to making a choice. What do you choose? We challenge you to do whatever it is you can do today that's going to make the situation better for you. Don't just dream it. Take action and do it. Debt will wash away if you're focused on abundance and on taking action to move ahead with ease.

We're going to help you with goal setting, which is an important component of success that many people think they've mastered when in fact they have not. This is an area that both of us have a lot of experience in and a lot of success with, and it comes down to being aligned with your deep desires and what you're passionate about.

Sometimes that will require you to create stretch goals. Sometimes a goal may require too much of a stretch or not enough. You may feel that you don't know how you're going to get there, but you should buy into it and believe in it.

We'll show you how to take a simple idea and initiate action to turn it into a business. One such success story I often refer to, illustrating how people can make money online with a simple idea, concerns an Irish man who had attended a funeral in the United States. The deceased was of Irish heritage, and many of the funeral attendees were Irish Americans. They were just about to put the casket in the ground when someone said, "I wish I had some Irish dirt to throw on top of that casket." That comment sparked an idea: dirt from Ireland sold to Irish Americans so that they could throw it on their burial grounds or on caskets or sprinkle it in their backyards.

They could keep it in a jar in the kitchen to remind them of their ancestral land.

In his first year of business, this fellow sold 528,000 pounds of Irish dirt and generated over $1 million. I suspect that he didn't have a clue about what steps needed to be taken. He started with an idea and took action. He put it out there in the world. He took a chance on himself and his idea, and it paid off. You can do this, too.

Stay open to those sorts of ideas as you're reading this book. You're going to hear about our experiences and other people's experiences. Our hope is that they will spark an idea of your own and inspire you to take a chance on yourself.

We'll also talk about having a commitment to growth. Anyone who has ever achieved anything in his or her life, who now enjoys success, is 100 percent committed to growth. These people recognize that you are either growing or dying. This isn't just about financial and business growth; it also refers to personal growth. We will show you how you can stay committed to growth while using strategies that enable you to enjoy your freedom and make the entire process extremely easy.

We're going to reveal daily practices that will get you and keep you on track so that you become much more efficient at what you choose to do. We identify and focus on specific disciplines that can absolutely, completely, and totally change your life in 24 hours or less.

One of our goals is to motivate you to step out and really take a look at your income generation from a different perspective so that you can try new ways to succeed. Not everything is going to work, but by trying new, radical, completely out of the box approaches, you can quantum jump your income and your business from where it is now to where you want it to be.

This book is not intended only for entrepreneurs and business owners; we also wrote it for those who have lost control of their income and want to regain direction and reassert control.

Wayne Dyer sumed up what we offer quite well: "Change the way you look at things, and the things you look at will change."

Ask yourself, starting right now, "What can I do today that my future self will thank me for?"

Our answer—and our pledge—to you is to read this book from beginning to end, do the exercises, and follow our steps and advice. It's that easy.

One day you will thank yourself because your business will have benefited from your emotional investment, and the resulting dividends will last a lifetime.

Let's get started!

Success Tools

Throughout the book you will find practical, success-enhancing tools that Brian and I use regularly that will assist you in creating goals, monitoring your progress, and bringing those goals to fruition.

Gratitude journal: This is a blank journal in which you write down every day what you are grateful for on that day. It can be that you are grateful for the people in your life, for the money you are making, or just for feeling energetic and healthy. The intention is to attract more good into your life.

Goal card: This is an index card on which you write your goals in the present tense. For instance, you could write, "I am building a successful business worth X dollars with every step I make every day." Keep your goal card in a pocket you use regularly, perhaps next to your wallet, so that you are always touching it and keeping the goal in the forefront of your mind.

Power life script: This is a visualization script that inspires emotion and is written in the present tense as though you were already living the life you want and have achieved the goals you set. Its length is up to you. It can be one paragraph or 15 pages long. Record it and listen to it every day.

Manifestation movie: Created as a PowerPoint presentation, this includes affirmations pulled out of your power life script using "I am" statements, inspiring quotes, and images. Feel free to add music. Watch it every day for five minutes or so. It's another tool to anchor you in the emotions of having what you desire, and it enables you to connect with gratitude.

Accountability list: Each week, create a list of goals for the week. Examples: have all my client meetings be fun, enjoyable, and productive; walk a mile each day; and eat only healthy food. Share this with an accountability partner.

Accomplishment list: This is used in tandem with an accountability list. Refer back to the previous week and rate how you did in meeting the goals you set for yourself.

DARN
EASY

PART I

Attitudes for Success Made Easy

The secret of change is to focus all of your energy, not on fighting the old, but on building the new.

—SOCRATES

Life Is NOT Meant to Be Hard

Don't plan yourself to death. Plan but remain flexible. Once you determine the kind of business that is right for you to build, don't overcomplicate things. Set forth action steps. You don't need to have all the steps covered to start a business. Attitude is the key to making it easy or complicated.

Don't Fight the Old, Build the New

If you are always looking back at past negative results, afraid you will repeat them, that's all you will keep attracting to yourself. Step forward with action into the new. Project yourself into the place you want to be. If you want different results, build new belief systems. Break old toxic habits; create new healthy ones.

Make a Decision to SHIFT Your Energy to Ease

When you shift into ease, you allow the positive to come. You attract what you need to you. Wearing rose-colored glasses sometimes is useful. Making a decision to shift your energy to ease is a starting point to all great results. Shifting is a matter of choice. Find people who will help you make the shift. You become who you surround yourself with.

A Philosophy Behind ANY Success

Have a clear mission statement. What are you going to contribute to the world? Where is the need or want for your service or product? Can you create value that will provide that contribution? How can you be of service and bring value to others? Do you have passion for what you're doing? Does your business provide you with emotional income? What is it you can give your clients for free that will grow your business?

From Mediocre to Magnificent

You see yourself either in abundance or wallowing in debt. Make sure that everything you do, you do to the best of your ability. Live every day with excellence. Doing this makes a big difference. Use your enthusiasm to bring your life up a notch. Successful businesses are based on caring about providing more value to affect people in positive ways.

Making Money Is a Habit You Develop

Go with the current of making money. The way you think and the relationships you cultivate reinforce the habit. Making money with ease is about adopting an abundance mentality. People line up in support of those who have a vision. Simple ideas can be the biggest moneymakers.

A Reality Check You Need to Cash

Be a dreamer *and* a doer. Positive thinking without action does little to advance your goals. Visualize the obstacles that may stand in your way. Identify the behaviors you need to overcome those obstacles. Use visualization to see yourself taking action and melting away the obstacles to success.

Choose Your Words Carefully

Create the mental foundation by using a higher state of awareness for business success. Is your self-talk empowering or sabotaging you? Choose your words carefully and mindfully. Start an awareness journal and make daily notes. Notice your thoughts and feelings, your self-talk, and your language in conversations with others. Would you do business with someone who talked to you the way you talk to yourself?

Your Darn Easy Assignment #1: Prevent Self-Sabotage

Your Darn Easy Assignment #2: Visualize Obstacles Melting Away

Life Is NOT Meant to Be Hard

By his own admission, James Hahn didn't have the focus or commitment to be a successful pro golfer. He spent too much time partying and goofing off with his buddies. He didn't push himself or try harder. The 33-year-old worked in a shoe store and struggled to make ends meet as he dabbled in his golf hobby. He had become skilled at making life hard when it should have come easy.

Most of us have had aha! moments that could be life-changing if only we took action to capitalize on the opportunity the epiphany presented. One of those moments came for Hahn during a PGA TOUR Canada event in Edmonton when he was trying to figure out how he could borrow money to pay his caddie and buy a plane ticket home to California.

"It just kind of hit me," Hahn explained in an interview with PGATOUR.com. "Hey, you have an opportunity to do something with your life."

That realization alone carried him farther in this tournament than he had ever finished before: eighth place for $3,000 in winnings. That more than covered the cost of his caddie and a plane ticket home.

In the aftermath, Hahn set about changing his thinking about success. He created his own program of positive thinking. "I would write down on a sticky note, 'I will putt great today,' and I put that everywhere, right next to my toothbrush, on the mirror in the bathroom, on the toilet seat, everywhere." Before each tournament he repeated a mantra: "I will putt great tomorrow. I will putt great tomorrow."

He fortified his mind with positive thoughts, and that translated into a heightened focus and skill level. He had suffered financially until he made that choice to shift his thinking and determine where best to invest his time and focus. His professional fortunes steadily turned around until in early 2015 he won his first PGA TOUR Tournament, the Northern Trust Open, which landed him a playing position in the Master's Tournament and a well-deserved introduction to the public spotlight.

This anecdote has universal applications and lessons far beyond the game of golf, especially for those who want financial independence to flow from their entrepreneurial endeavors.

Hahn's story of achievement illustrates a powerful point that is a central theme of this book: shift your focus, exercise your choice to have a more positive attitude, take the necessary actions, and you will experience the ease of getting results you may never have dreamed possible. It's that simple. It can be that easy.

Being a successful entrepreneur and business owner starts in your mind and with the beliefs and thoughts you *choose* to guide your decisions and your interactions with others.

Don't Fight the Old, Build the New

I t's been said that the secret of change is to focus all your energy not on fighting the old but on building the new. That's really what we're doing in *Darn Easy*.

Every day, as we wake up, we have an opportunity to make a new decision about what we are going to focus on. What are we going to create today?

Project yourself into the place where you want to be. Visualize how you have achieved the goal. Here's an illustration of how that works in practice, taken from my own experience.

We had our house up for sale (this was several houses ago). As I stood at the front window of my home, I saw the "For Sale" sign on my lawn and felt overwhelming anxiety. I couldn't believe that the house hadn't sold yet even though we had dropped the price. It got to the point where our agent told us that because the house had been on the market for so long, people were wondering what was wrong with it.

There was nothing wrong with the house. We just decided that we didn't want to have that home anymore. We wanted to move. As

I stood there feeling doubt about whether we would ever sell it, I caught myself and thought, "Hey, wait a minute. This is not going to help me. What would I like to experience instead?"

I called our real estate agent and asked him to come over with a "Sold" sign that I could plant in our yard. He was surprised and confused. "But your house hasn't sold yet," he blurted.

I told him I knew that. But I wanted that sign anyway. I had something in mind.

He came over with the sign, and I took a picture of it in our front yard. I printed out a digital photo of the sign and put it on my desk as a reminder of my goal.

My neighbors saw the agent with the "Sold" sign, and you know how neighbors can be; they all rushed over asking if I had really sold my house. I explained that it was a visualization exercise. That was not the response they were expecting.

The sign came down, and my agent left. About three weeks later, we had sold the house, much to our agent's and our neighbors' surprise. That was after it had been on the market for at least a year. Call it a coincidence or whatever you want, but I firmly believe the shift in our fortunes came from the visualization ritual.

The change and shift in focus I made was to take action and say, "Okay, that's not what I choose to see. I want to see this as a done deal." What helped me anchor the vision and goal was seeing that "Sold" sign on my lawn.

You can either imagine the achievement of your goal, keeping it fixed in your mind and regularly reflecting on it as if it had already happened, or you can take an actual picture of it as I did and keep that vision posted in front of you to reflect and meditate on.

The key thing is to take action toward your goal both in your mind and in your activities. Visualizing the completion of your goal isn't a substitute for taking action, yet it's an indispensable part of any success that involves overcoming obstacles. Visualization isn't passive. It's your mind taking action.

Brian and I see so many people who have a business they want to start who just plan and then plan some more. They continue to plan until they plan themselves to death. That's often a sign of fear and insecurity, with the fear being that if they don't plan for every single minor detail, something will go wrong and they won't know how to fix it.

This isn't to say that you shouldn't plan, at least somewhat and within reason. Just don't overplan to the point where you do nothing; you need to take action. That action should always begin with the completion of your goal fixed firmly in your mind.

Initiate whatever it is you want and need to do, even if it's just taking little baby steps, to make some progress toward your goal. Every day you take a step forward, visualize the completion of the goal and feel what it will be like when that happens.

We speak from experience when we say it's unbelievable what you will and can accomplish if you put this method to use in service of your desires.

Make a Decision to SHIFT Your Energy to Ease

A lady who cleaned houses for a living once told me that her husband was constantly negative. He was negative about everything and everyone. That was a revelation that surprised me because she was one of the happiest people I had ever met. She always seemed to be singing and smiling. She also happened to be very reliable.

I couldn't resist asking her, "How can you sleep in the same bed with this really miserable guy and remain unaffected by it?"

"I just look at him as an example of what not to be like," she replied.

Even though she loved him and had made a decision to stay with him despite his toxic state of mind, she managed to remain unaffected and to use his attitude as a cautionary example.

She had made a conscious decision to shift where she directed the energy of her attention. That's a really important quality to have, especially if you're starting a business and few of the people in your life are supportive of your efforts.

One of my personal practices has been to shift the focus from the negative over to the positive whenever I become aware of negativity. I have found over time, with a lot of practice, that I've became a lot better at that.

It's important never to allow negativity to drag you down. You have a choice about whether you allow that to happen.

There is a story Bob Proctor shares about a couple who wanted to buy real estate. Bob asked them, "Have you decided to buy the home? Have you made that decision? Have you committed yourself?"

They started giving Bob all the reasons why they hadn't committed and why buying a house couldn't work for them. "We don't have the money" was their big reason.

"You don't need the money," Bob replied.

"What do you mean we don't need the money?" the couple exclaimed, unable to believe what they were hearing. "Of course you need the money to buy real estate."

Bob explained to them the simple principle that when you've made a decision about what you want, that's where and when things start to happen. Then you will begin to attract to you the money required to achieve your goal.

That shift happens when you make the conscious decision, adopt that attitude of faith and commitment, and reach out to take the necessary action. Whether you will achieve your goal is a choice, and it begins with your attitude.

We're Inviting You to Make the Decision to Shift into Ease

We urge you to make the shift because it's a choice we all have, and the more often you make that choice, the easier and the more of a habit it becomes.

When Brian and I wake up in the morning, we decide the day is going to be an easy day. Today I'm going to enjoy myself. Today I'm going to create more. I'm going to give more. I'm going to love more. I'm going to experience more in my life. It's a choice that we're always making. You can make it, too.

There is only one person who is creating chaos in your life right now: you. You need to decide if you want to continue down this road of difficulty, chaos, and anxiety or want to stop and take a breath and choose to focus on having this be a productive but enjoyable day. Constantly keep in mind that everything we do, everything we experience, and every way we react is a choice we make. When we're going through anything, we step back for one second and just ask, "What am I choosing here? Am I choosing difficult and chaotic, or am I choosing ease?" Ask yourself, "What can I do in this moment that can shift this experience to ease? How can I make this day and situation much more enjoyable?"

Every time you step back and choose ease, it flows. It flows like water from a faucet you've turned on.

Shifting is the starting point for all sustainable success. When you consciously make a decision to amplify and crank up your energy, it's primed for what we call a "vibrational" state of attraction.

In our experience, there are a few techniques well worth trying to keep you in alignment with shifting into ease of being.

Find People Who Will Help You Shift

Identify the people in your life you can talk to who will help you switch into a positive state of mind. Whether it's a good friend or someone else you trust, open up and tell that person what you're looking for. Explain how he or she can help you make those switches in attitude and approach.

Surround Yourself with Positive, Like-Minded People

If you surround yourself with people who aren't really doing anything with their lives, who exist without clear goals, you may become just like them. At the very least, you will be influenced by them.

If you surround yourself with people who are out there pursuing their goals and building businesses by taking action, you will become like them. At the very least, you will be inspired by them.

What you attract is really what you are. You do become who you surround yourself with. In building a business, you can often feel alone. I work from home, and that can be rather isolating, but I have a team of people I can count on who work for me and who I know are action-oriented movers and shakers. I exercise my choice to refuse to work with people who are listless and uninspired.

Adopt that point of view, look around, and ask yourself, "Who am I surrounding myself with? Who are my friends? Who do I work with? Are these people I want to work with and do business with? Do I like what they are doing?" If the answer to all of these questions is yes, you are going about it in the right way.

You Also Need to Have Fun

Let's face it, we all have our bad days, those times when it's a challenge to be our usual inspiring selves. But if you find a way to shift and enjoy the moment despite these momentary challenges, people are going to be attracted naturally to you. They will be curious about how you manage to be so upbeat.

When you handle your business in that way, you are going to attract more clients and associates just because they want to be around you. That may sound kind of odd, but it's a really important thing to master in initiating or sustaining the success of a business.

Having fun and injecting more joy into your life is really important for business success, or any kind of success for that matter. Even if you're going through what seems like a dark day or a challenging time in your life, how you choose to surmount that obstacle and instead turn it into a fun experience helps define how resilient and magnetic you are.

If you're worried about your business and what you're going to do and how you're going to perform, you are focused only on you. You're not focused on your customer or what it is that you want to accomplish with your business. You're not having fun, and neither are the customers when they're around you.

The more you can inspire people to laugh, smile, and feel good about you, themselves, and life, the better that experience will be for them and of course for you and your business. You're going to find that you'll enjoy everything you do so much more, and so will everyone in contact with you. You will attract more clients and friends.

A Philosophy Behind
ANY Success

If you aren't making a difference in other people's lives,
you shouldn't be in business—it's that simple.

—RICHARD BRANSON

B rian started a program over a decade ago called Insight of the Day. It was a way to stay in touch with clients by sending out inspirational quotes and an uplifting story every Friday. But it evolved into something much bigger and quite lucrative.

If he had known what was required to put this idea into place and to get that aspect of his business going, he admits, he probably would never have done it. But he was brought up cultivating the mindset that if you have a dream and want to do something toward your goals, you've got to take the initiative, step out with confidence, and just start doing it.

When he first started Insight of the Day, people told him what a crazy idea it was and asked, "How will you ever earn money from inspirational quotes?"

We all know people who will tell you all the reasons why you can't do something. Just once, do what others say you can't do, and you will never pay attention to their attempts to place limitations on you again.

That is a key consideration because no matter what goal you are pursuing, you're always going to encounter negative people. If you maintain focus and drive toward what you want to do, you must also summon the will to ignore their opinions because they're not going to do you any good.

If people have objective opinions that can help you improve what you're building, that's great and useful. If they are being negative because that's their nature and it's shutting you down, you need to walk away. In many instances, it's family members who act this way. If you share your goals with them, they will think you're crazy because they believe they know you—at least the old you. Share your goals only with those you know will be supportive and on your side no matter what.

Whenever you start a business, you obviously have to go into it focused on how to make a profit and earn an income. With Insight of the Day, Brian's primary focus was on developing something called *emotional income.*

He got the idea for Insight of the Day from small books full of inspirational quotes and uplifting stories that were sent out in the 1970s and 1980s as part of a monthly or quarterly subscription. From Monday to Thursday, Brian sent inspirational quotes. Every Friday, he sent an uplifting story. His intention was to affect or touch people's lives that day and prompt them to look at their experiences in a slightly different way.

He started receiving positive responses from people who had been going through rough times, whether it was a relationship breakup, business challenges, an illness, or death. One quote or one story changed the way they looked at what they were experiencing. Their enthusiastic responses made Brian aware that he was touching people's lives. That's what we call emotional income.

It's so important that whatever you do, whatever type of income you choose to generate, you find something that will earn you a profit *and* generate emotional income from doing it. If you receive that emotional income, believe us when we say that everything will fall into place. You will have an incredibly satisfying business. If you go into it really caring about what you're doing and you get that emotional income as a result, everything else you desire will follow.

Be of Service to Others

Commit to be of service to others with your business. Make that your mantra. Make it your passion.

I've noticed that when I'm on a call with someone who is interested in working with me and I say to this person, "How may I serve?" or "How may I be of service to you today?" it's met with pleasant surprise. Most people are attracted to that idea. It's a powerful mindset to create and practice to employ. It will reverberate and help your business in ways you can't measure.

We invite you to initiate such a shift. We invite you to shift into ease right now. Decide that your life is going to be easy and that you are open to it being that way even if you find yourself saying, "I don't know how to do it, Peggy and Brian. I understand what you're saying, but I don't know how."

Just open up and choose to say instead, "I'm willing to have this experience happen. I'm open to the change and I'm here; I'm committed to this. I'm going to have my life be easy. My life is easy right now."

That is what it takes: a choice, a decision. There is so much power in making a decision to do something, especially when it's to your own benefit.

Determine What You Can Give Your Clients for Free

Make it something that's going to help your clients and create a relationship between you and them that will grow your business. When you do that and do it successfully, you will be amazed at how your business can prosper.

There are many different ways to get creative and put your services or products out there. But how do you drive Internet traffic? Giving something for free can accomplish that.

Through Brian, I met Anik Singal, who wanted guidance about a book he intended to write, *The Circle of Profit,* about how to turn your passion, hobby, and expertise into a million-dollar digital business.

Anik wanted a New York publishing house and a *New York Times* bestseller. Of course, every author does, and some are willing and financially able to hire companies that guarantee, in return for hundreds of thousands of dollars, that they will make a book a bestseller. I advised Anik against taking that expensive and risky approach.

Publishers want authors with a following, a visible platform. Anik had that platform already, and so he wrote the book, self-published it, posted it online, and reached out to his audience and invited them to download it for free over several days. People eagerly responded to the offer, and 20,000 e-books were downloaded during those few days. He increased his business visibility as a result of this offer.

This is an example of another darn easy approach to building a business: give away something that is of value to your customers.

It's important, of course, to have an awareness of your customers' or clients' needs even if they don't necessarily know what those needs are themselves. The key to learning what they need or want is to stay in contact with them.

During Brian's real estate days, he was a big financial success because he stayed in touch with his past clients. It's amazing how many real estate agents don't do that. To this day, it just dumbfounds

Brian and me that such an obvious opportunity is so often over-looked. Brian always sends something to his past clients and potential clients to maintain that essential contact.

The one thing you really need to consider seriously when you're starting or building a business is creating an e-mail database of your clients that consists at the very least of their names and e-mail addresses. Find a simple way and a good reason to contact them periodically and offer them something of value for free. If it's an e-mail newsletter, for example, it can't be very long. Otherwise, they won't read it with consistency. Keep it short and simple.

From Mediocre to Magnificent

B rian and I attended a presentation on how to get business prospects and convert them into sales. The presenters kept confusing
the audience with unfamiliar or complicated terminology, apparently
in an attempt to be viewed as knowledgeable. For instance, they used
the term *trip wire* without defining it. They gave us a seven-step system, but I got stuck on step 2 because I was trying to figure out what
it meant. What could have been a magnificent presentation quickly
turned mediocre.

Always keep in mind that people need basic and simple terms to
relate to and apply. If you are guiding people, don't get fancy or try
to be too clever. Communicate your message so that people really get
it. Explain your process at a fifth-grade level. Don't overcomplicate
it because that will trip you up.

Being magnificent at what you do isn't about ego and projecting
false impressions. It's about embracing an authentic state of mind
that is based on service to others.

You See Yourself Either in Abundance or Wallowing in Debt

You will attract more of whatever it is you choose to see. I'm not going to say I see myself in abundance 100 percent of the time, yet I know for a fact that I focus on that the majority of the time.

It all comes back to a choice. What do you choose?

You could be in debt right now, and if that's the case, it's even more important to focus on the theme of abundance and the good that is coming to you and that you deserve.

Then take action. Do whatever it is that you can do today to improve your situation for tomorrow. Don't just dream it. Do it.

Debt will wash away if you're focused on abundance and on taking action to move ahead.

Cultivate an abundance mentality. Brian and I know a young man named Avi who's in his early twenties and earns more than $1 million a year, something that is rare among people that age.

Avi created some wonderful conditioning habits and belief systems around abundance. In 2013, his goal was to make $20 million. I saw Avi at the Science of Getting Rich Event in Los Angeles and asked him, "I know your goal is to make twenty million dollars this year. How are you going to do it?" He responded with a snap of his fingers. "Easily," he said.

Everyone can learn a lesson from Avi. He is the epitome of what we're talking about in this book. It all comes naturally to him.

He demonstrates how you can earn a decent income doing anything if you put your mind to it. Avi sells furnaces to homeowners. This young man has an incredible work ethic and has one of the best personalities I have ever come across. Every time I see Avi, he's wearing the biggest smile. You want to be around this fellow. He is attracting business into his life. He also gets out there and takes action. He's up early in the morning, quite literally knocking on people's doors to drum up business. He's out doing whatever it takes to earn an incredible income, and he is succeeding at it.

Condition Yourself with New Positive Habit Patterns

Go from "No, I can't do it" to "Yes, I can do it." Otherwise, the doubts will creep up and overwhelm you.

When you're feeling that doubt or fear rise, the best suggestion I can make is to do something in that moment that will further your cause or your business. Take action. In doing that, you will find your confidence.

Over time, as you apply these suggestions and create these patterns of discipline in your beliefs and attitudes, you condition yourself so that it becomes an automatic response the next time a challenge comes along.

It takes practice to forge that state of mind so that it becomes automatic. One thing I do to help with the process is to post reminders around me constantly. They may be affirmations, questions, or goals that will restore me to an abundant frame of mind.

Throughout the early part of my life, I was constantly in search of what would make a difference in the trajectory of my career. I came to realize that one factor was being aware of what my thoughts were and basing choices on what I was thinking. Gaining clarity and making clearer goals made a big difference in my life.

Also, I realized that connecting to gratitude is so powerful because it's an energetic experience of tapping into the law of vibration and, through that, the law of attraction, which would bring more of the good into my life. It could be that putting fun into your life is going to be the one thing that makes all the difference for you. Or it may be the feeling that comes from your contributions to the greater good. Or it could be a combination of realizations that provide that big push to success.

Remember, the essential step is the transformation of your attitudes and beliefs. The next step is to surround yourself with people who will encourage you and fuel you with the advice and inspiration and support you need to move forward with confidence.

Step up and do something, because if you sit back and focus on the doubt and the worry that it won't work—it won't work. Keep asking yourself, "What can I do right now that's going to take me one step farther in the direction I need to be going?" It doesn't matter how small the step is; take it. Every time you do that, you will be farther away from doubt.

Avoid Becoming Scattered

Step back and make that choice to shift into ease when you find yourself getting scattered. Scattered behaviors mirror a scattered mind.

Recognize if you have this tendency and monitor the impact it's having on your business and your business relations. If it's become a problem, take action and exercise choice. Step back and change this chaotic pattern. Ask for help if you need it.

Every time I go to bed at night, I've got a lot of different things going on, many different projects I am juggling at one time. It wouldn't be hard to become scattered. I have found that the easiest way to clear my head is to take a piece of paper and write down all the important tasks that I need to accomplish the next day. That way, I don't have to worry about them. I don't dream about them at night. I don't fret and worry. I go to sleep with ease.

When I wake up in the morning, I take my list, start from the top, and go through the items one by one. It's amazing how much you can get done this way. Over time, being scattered becomes much less of a problem.

Practice the Power of Gratitude

Before I start my first task every morning, I sit down and give thanks in my gratitude journal. There are items in it that make multiple appearances: my family, our health, the love and connection that we have. I write down things that haven't happened yet, but I write them down as if they had already taken place. Part of my reason for engaging in this ritual is to put myself in a place of awareness so that I more easily notice my patterns of thought, my self-talk, and how I speak to others.

In Brian's case, he has a gratitude rock. It's a tiny stone that says "gratitude" on it that he keeps on his desk right beside his computer at home. Every morning, he holds it and thinks of everything in his life for which he is grateful.

What an empowering and incredible way to start the day! It puts your whole being at ease so that you can attract more incredible people and situations to you.

Experience gratitude all the time, every day. Experience it as often as you possibly can.

You have a goal. You have this end vision of where you want to be. Keep picturing that vision. Be grateful for being in that position.

The more often you can get into that state of mind, the more empowered you are to manifest the reality you want. Practicing consistent expressions of gratitude helps increase your level of confidence in your performance and your faith in the positive outcomes coming your way.

Making Money Is a
Habit You Develop

Bob Proctor once said that if you look at successful people closely, one thing you notice is how they are in the habit of making money. The way you are thinking, the relationships you establish—all this helps create and reinforce the habit.

My current husband, Denis, and I were having a conversation before we were married, and I remember him asking me, "What happens when you're not making money?" My reaction was like that of a dog that tilts its head, not comprehending what was said. I didn't understand the question at all, but I understood that there must be something underlying it. Why was he asking?

I replied, "First of all, I've never been in a situation of not making money. I always make money. There might have been dry spells and more abundant times and times of more valleys than hills, but I've always been making money."

What his question made me realize is that making money and attracting money into your life becomes a habit. Making money is a *habit you develop*. If I'm not making money, I'll find ways to make money. It's an abundance mentality.

It's a powerful concept to help you understand the ease of things. People will line up behind people who have a vision. Go with the current of making money. You might get stuck in the current's rocks sometimes, but you know instinctively how to get out. You constantly invest to learn more to deliver more. As with any habit, you do it automatically. If you're always focused on making money, you will make that happen.

Among the things I love about making money on the Internet is how easy it is and how you can do it in the comfort of your home no matter where you are in the world as long as you have Internet access. There was a gentleman who was an executive and had a pretty busy life. He found that he often lost, misplaced, or wore holes in his socks but that he didn't have time to buy new ones. He came up with the idea of a sockscription, a subscription to men's socks. He knew many businessmen would be interested in a subscription service that would deliver socks to their home regularly so that they never would have to go out and buy them again.

For many, this might seem like a ridiculous idea, but he set up a website, began marketing it, and within a very short period had 60,000 members paying $89 for an annual sockscription. That's more than $5 million a year in income. It was a simple idea that met a need and provided him with a healthy income with ease.

How many people actually practice a belief system built around how easy it is to make money? Not many. Most seem to think that making money outside a nine-to-five job is difficult and beyond their ability. They don't grasp that the mastery of self-employment is really just a shift in thinking.

Napoleon Hill once said that when money comes in quantities known as "big money," it flows to the one who accumulates it as easily as water flows downhill. This is in alignment with knowing and having that ease and practicing a belief system that helps make it so.

Hill goes on to say that there exists a great unseen stream of power that is like a river except that one side flows in one direction, carrying all who get into that side of the stream onward and upward to wealth. The other side flows in the opposite direction, carrying all who are unfortunate enough to get trapped in it to misery and poverty.

Which river are you in? Which river do you choose to be in?

If you're in the upward river, you're in the unseen stream of power or movement toward abundance. This book will help you get into that mindset of journeying onward and upward to success and wealth.

We all wrestle periodically with doubts. Years ago, I remember getting to a point in my life at which I thought that maybe all this positive thinking just didn't work. That was poison. Cultivating and holding on to such doubts will contaminate your results like pouring poison on a living plant.

From experience and observation, I realized that the premise, ideas, philosophies, and universal laws all work as advertised. You need only embrace them and take action. You've got to see yourself living in abundance, knowing that it's easy to attract money to you, that it's yours for the asking and the taking.

A Reality Check You
Need to Cash

B e a dreamer *and* a doer. You cannot engage in wishful or positive thinking without also taking action to make your dreams and goals a reality. There are no magic wands to wave. There is no Wizard of Oz to grant your wishes.

Yes, you must be a dreamer to be successful, but you must also take action. It is the dreamers that take action who make a difference in this world.

The one big missing piece in the movie and book *The Secret* about the law of attraction was that once you have a dream that you visualize, you must *also* take action and the steps necessary to make your goal or desire a reality.

To illustrate our point, a psychology professor at New York University, Gabriele Oettingen, did numerous studies over several decades examining how positive thinking by itself does little to advance, much less achieve, your goals. In fact, merely thinking or dreaming about your future makes you less likely to achieve anything. In her words, "Just dreaming, detached from an awareness of reality, actually saps the energy we need to perform the hard work of meeting the challenges we face in real life."

How does she propose that we remain positive yet stay motivated and prepare ourselves for the challenges ahead? First of all, our wishful thinking needs to be accompanied by a realistic assessment of the obstacles that could stand in our way. It's a reality check process she calls "mental contrasting," which she describes this way: "It instructs us to dream our dreams, but then visualize the personal barriers that prevent us from achieving them. My studies show that when we perform such mental contrasting, we actually gain energy to take action. And when we go farther and specify the actions we intend to take as obstacles arise, we energize ourselves even more."

Not only does mental contrasting help keep us from getting overwhelmed by life, especially by the unexpected twists and turns of events and situations, but "the obstacles we think most impede us from realizing our deepest wishes can actually hasten their fulfillment."

As evidence for her theory, Professor Oettingen cites a study involving college students whose brain responses were monitored as they engaged in either fantasizing about their desired goal or fantasizing and then engaging in mental contrasting to see the obstacles and how they could be overcome. Fantasy failed to activate the areas of the brain connected to memory and willful action, whereas mental contrasting lit up those areas.

This study demonstrated that positive fantasies don't automatically translate into motivated behaviors. You must add strong determination and commitment to your own visual process of implementing your wishes by identifying likely obstacles and the behaviors you need to circumvent them.

Choose Your Words Carefully

A prominent cardiologist in the Los Angeles area, Dr. Cynthia Thaik, provides us with an example of how the language we choose to use—whether in our heads while talking to ourselves or in the way we speak with others—really does make a difference in achieving our goals.

During the summer of 2012, Dr. Thaik began experimenting with the idea that your thoughts can transform your reality. She created a generic vision statement to use in an attempt to turn around the fortunes of her medical practice. Referrals and overall business had dropped off dramatically, and she was experiencing anxiety and stress over that reversal.

The generic vision statement she initially created wasn't working as she had hoped, and so I advised her to rewrite it because the more clarity and specifics you have, the more you will receive back. I call this a *power life script* that emphasizes the use of positive, specific, emotionally descriptive words.

She worked on eliminating both negative thoughts and negative verbal statements from her vocabulary while listening to her revised vision statement every day, which emphasized what she was grateful for in her life and clarified how she would be of service to her clients.

Here are some excerpts she provided me from her vision statement:

"I, Cynthia Thaik, feel the elation and the gratitude of easily and smoothly achieving and enjoying all of my goals. All of my success comes easily to me. I am happy with who I am. I love myself. I appreciate myself, and I treat myself in a loving way.

"I have plenty of money to do whatever I want to do. I have an abundance of money in my bank accounts. I am positively serving the world with my gifts and in a way that is beneficial and contributing at a high level. I show up every day in service of my highest good. I love my deep, meaningful, powerful interactions with my patients. Every encounter creates tremendous shifts in my patients and leaves them feeling deeply connected with me and richly inspired. I attract a minimum of 10 new cardiology clients each day, 10 new wellness clients each week, from various sources, many referring physicians, including many self-referrals that seek me out specifically for my integrative holistic style. I hold the intention of service very reverently."

Within just a few months of using this new vision statement, Dr. Thaik began seeing improvements in the volume of new client referrals and the success of her medical practice. "It has become easy," she told me.

"My medical practice turned around," Dr. Thaik explained. "I had been really stressed by the financial challenge, and this vision statement helped me relieve the stress. That reverberated throughout my relationships. I got many more clients as a result. And my marriage and relationships with my three children were all strengthened. I got more ease and flow and mental clarity. Even my intuition improved."

"I realize this is an ongoing process," Dr. Thaik continued. "I have the awareness that even when future roadblocks come and I wonder where did the magic go, I know the flow of ease can return. I have faith now that no matter what may come in changes to the landscape of the medical profession, what is in my control are the feelings of gratitude and generosity of service, and that will keep me on track."

Cut the Weeds from Your Speech

Have you ever noticed how sometimes you will think or say, "I know this is going to be really hard," or "I have no idea how I'm ever going to do that."

The words you use can have a huge impact on whether you're experiencing ease or difficulty in your life. Your words can become self-fulfilling prophecies.

On one occasion, I arrived at my sister's home in Toronto to stay for the night. She was getting her house ready for sale. She was purging closets and cupboards of unnecessary things. At one point she said to me, "This move is going to be a nightmare." My response to her was, "If you choose for it to be, it will be, but that is up to you." I stopped her negative thought process in that moment.

This is something I often do as I'm having conversations with clients. I will interject, "What did you just say?"

Your words are so powerful. They are energy in motion. If you say that you're sick and tired, you're more likely to become sick and tired. If you say it's going to be hard, it becomes hard. If you say it's going to be a nightmare, what do you end up experiencing? Maybe it's not always negative, but the energy expended in what you say often shapes or determines your eventual experience.

It comes back to word choice again. Much of the time I think most people go through the day on autopilot. They don't even realize what they are saying and doing to themselves. The first step is to be really aware of our self-talk.

Self-Talk Needs to Be Empowering

If it's not empowering, self-talk is not going to help us deal with the situations that arise. If we're looking to grow a business and create better relationships, we really need to monitor our self-talk and alter it as necessary. Even during rough patches when you may not have many great experiences, there has to be something good you can find in your life to focus on and use in your self-talk.

Once, when Brian had to speak in front of a large group of people and was feeling nervous about it, his father advised him: "If you're nervous before you get up there, what you're focusing on is what people will think of you; you're not focusing on how you can help them." It was like a smack across the face for Brian. Now whenever he feels any nerves, he goes back to making that choice about how he wants to feel.

You have to be consciously aware of what you're doing to yourself. I go into myself and think, "What can I do to help somebody? What message can I relay that will take somebody to a better place?" When I do that exercise, the nerves just go away. If we're always focused on the right things, our self-talk becomes better and our lives become better.

Nervousness isn't always going to disappear, but we learn how to manage it or how to accept it. Brian had that shift. He began to focus not on the discomfort he feels but on what he can do that is of value.

Your audience happens to be your clients and customers. Stop worrying about what they're going to think of you and your performance. Choose to switch and stay focused on what you can give them that will be of value.

Your Darn Easy Assignment #1
Prevent Self-Sabotage

Going forward, we invite you to begin paying attention to your language. Notice if you say anything that is destructive to your goals or that keeps you in a rut of difficulty rather than strolling down that street called ease.

Is your self-talk empowering or sabotaging you? Notice your thoughts and feelings and the language you use with others. Would you do business with someone who talked to you the way you talk to yourself?

Start with awareness

Awareness is the necessary starting point. Notice what you're observing. Become aware of the language you're using.

Keep an awareness journal and take daily notes to monitor and chronicle your negative thoughts, words, and deeds.

Work on eliminating negative words from your speech.

Notice if you say the word *hard*, as in "This will be really hard to do." Bite your tongue. Don't say, "It's going to be tough." Cancel that thought. Don't say, "This is going to be difficult. I can't do it."

Become very aware of the words that you choose to speak. Here is an easy-to-use three-step process:

1. Notice any negative feelings.
2. Decide to switch. Think to yourself, "This is not going to serve me. I have a choice about what kind of day I am going to experience." Decide in that moment to make a shift. You can switch.
3. Ask yourself, "What kind of day would I like to experience? Who is creating this experience right now?"

That awareness works in the moment, and it can continue to do so in your day-to-day experiences. It can also work more broadly as it relates to your goals and objectives. How am I going to do this? You notice it in that moment, and then you decide, "I'm going to choose to shift from that negative, unproductive energy."

Sometimes you can make the switch by stopping what you're doing and asking yourself, "What is it I'd like to experience right now, in the moment? What is that going to feel like?"

Next, tell yourself that it's going to feel great. It will be easy. You'll feel grateful. You'll feel joyful. You'll be celebrating. Make the choice to switch to those emotions right now.

Your Darn Easy Assignment #2
Visualize Obstacles Melting Away

Active visualization and guided imagery are two useful and powerful tools for relieving stress, anxiety, fear, doubt, and anything that sabotages you. These are practices that work to program your subconscious to summon at will positive thoughts and inspired feelings to help you overcome obstacles and achieve your goals.

Your imagination is a powerful tool that can be employed to initiate or accelerate all manner of healing, both physical and psychological. For example, at the Academy for Guided Imagery in California, therapists teach clinicians how to use guided imagery with patients to strengthen their immune systems and decrease stress and anxiety.

For our purposes, we give you several options. You don't need to sit alone quietly in a room to engage in active visualization. You can be moving around and engaged in your normal routine.

One type of visualization that I use frequently is the power life script exercise. I write out a script in which I visualize my goals and having achieved them. I describe the goals and how I feel about both the goals and myself. Then I record the entire script in the present tense and play it back to myself every day.

This script is particularly useful for me to listen to when I'm driving. A bonus: it makes the time spent driving go by much faster. You may also listen to your script through earphones as you take long mindful walks in nature or as you sit by the ocean or a peaceful pond.

A second visualization exercise that is more standard and widely practiced involves sitting alone quietly with your eyes closed. It's a form of meditation. Spend 10 to 15 minutes visualizing what it looks and feels like to overcome obstacles and achieve your goals. Imagine the obstacles one by one and see yourself in your mind's eye solving each problem with ease. You may also use a version of the power life script in the Appendix and meditate on the mental imagery that your words summon.

PART II

Aligning Goals with Your Desires

We gain strength and courage and confidence by each experience in which we really stop to look fear in the face. We must do that which we think we cannot.

—ELEANOR ROOSEVELT

The Universe Is Ready for You

Whatever you are prepared for is what the universe is prepared to give. If you're focused on the good, not just wishing but seeing the good outcomes you desire for your business, you've set the stage for positive results. Most people think the worst, and that is what they attract. When you see the vision of what you want and you feel it, you are in harmony with your goal and will attract it to you. Feel faith and trust that there is a desire for what you are bringing forth. Beware of scarcity conditioning.

Your Success Is Guaranteed

Don't allow yourself to get muddled by details. Every day, focus on how to accomplish something positive that day. Make this the best possible day it can be to make a difference in the life of your business. Make "My success is absolutely guaranteed" into a mantra. Repeat it to yourself every day. What would you do and how would you be if you knew you could not fail? Banish trepidation. Be fearless. Have faith in the outcome.

Get Out of Your Own Way

Make taking action a way of life. You are the only one standing in your own way. Cultivate a positive mindset. Develop an awareness of your thoughts and actions. Doing reflective meditation every day will help create that awareness. Pay attention to what you are feeling and thinking in the moment. Nourish your mind as well as your body every day to heighten awareness. Surround yourself with people who encourage you to be better and do better.

Outcome-Focused Consciousness

Focus on what you want, not on what you don't want. Create outcome-based mission statements and revenue plans. Every day, ask if something is moving you forward or away from your goals. It begins with producing and designing what other people will want to tell the world about. Carry a goal card. Act as if you'd already accomplished what you set for yourself. Set goals not for what you'll get but for who you become in reaching them.

Be Specific and Aim High

Goals can be personal or business-related. The more specific you are about what you want, the clearer the picture you have to move toward will be. What does a successful business really mean to you? Is it easily run, not requiring all of your time? Will you still have time for your family? How profitable do you want it to be? How much income do you want? Be specific. Aim high.

Uncomfortable Goals and Why They Work

Goals must inspire you. They should make you stretch. Set goals that move you out of your comfort zone. If you know exactly how to achieve a goal, your goal is probably too easy. If you see yourself with your goal, you can have it. What you learn through this process is invaluable. Stretch goals facilitate growth. It's not just the goal that's important; it's who you become in achieving it. You will strengthen qualities such as faith, trust, and joy. Make something goal-related happen today.

Polish the Language of Your Goals

Write down your goals in the present tense and think of them in the present tense. Act and feel as if you were already experiencing the goal's achievement. Use the present tense as if you were living it right now. Any word that sounds negative will feel negative. If you set a goal to eliminate debt, you are focused on debt and on feeling debt. Instead, think about how your bank account is bulging and your credit cards are paid off each month. Words are energy in motion. Grow the mental foundation for your business by using positive thoughts.

Your Darn Easy Assignment #1: Congratulate Yourself in Advance

Your Darn Easy Assignment #2: Getting Your Goals Straight

The Universe Is Ready for You

About 20 years ago, my husband and I decided to convert our relationship of a marriage to a divorce. That prompted me to set a goal. I was very clear that I was going to buy a home for me and our son, two-year-old Michel.

As part of my practice, I became really clear on what it was I wanted by writing on a goal card, "I am so happy and grateful to live in my beautiful four-bedroom home. It is professionally decorated. It's fully furnished. We live in a gorgeous neighborhood." I wrote all that down and became connected to what it would feel like to own that home.

Charles and I had put our own home up for sale. It was in the country. Houses in the country don't sell as quickly as do those in the city. We weren't getting any activity on our house whatsoever. Despite all that, I stayed focused on my goal, and I'd go look at homes for me and my son to buy once our other house sold.

When I set a goal, I don't have to know how it's going to happen. Everything doesn't have to be planned out. I just have to see myself in possession of what I desire. We lowered the price on our house several times, but months went by and nothing was happening. It seemed that I was stuck.

Meanwhile, I heard about this fund-raiser called the Dream of a Lifetime. It takes place once a year for the Children's Hospital of Eastern Ontario (CHEO). You could buy a ticket for $100. The prize: a beautiful fully furnished and decorated four-bedroom home in a wonderful neighborhood full of young children. You could go visit the home and buy tickets. I drove out to the house, and when I walked in, I realized that it was exactly what I had described on my goal card.

I bought a ticket. Then I changed my goal card to read "I, Peggy McColl, am so happy and so grateful now that my son, Michel, and I live in this beautiful home located at . . ." and put the house address on the goal card. I stepped into the whole experience of feeling what it would be like to live in the home.

This was my ritual. I would visualize going and sitting on the furniture in the family room, where I'd touch the furniture and feel the leather, and then I'd go into the living room and touch the furniture and feel the fabric of the couch. Then I'd go to the dining room and sit at the head of the table and imagine we were having our family Thanksgiving dinner, and I could see my sister passing the potatoes and really felt the experience. Then I would go upstairs, and I knew exactly which room would be my son's. I went down the hall to the master suite and sprawled on the bed and looked at the ceiling and imagined going to bed at night in my bedroom. I walked into the bathroom, and there was this huge Roman tub. I stepped into the tub and lay down and fully connected to what it would feel like to have a bubble bath in my Roman tub. I could literally smell the bath salts.

The draw finally came. I didn't win the house, but I knew not to throw away my goal. We can't dictate to the universe exactly how things are going to come to us. We can only look for ways and seize the opportunities when they are presented. We can stay open to the means, and we should take some action. But if it doesn't happen the exact way that we think it's going to happen, we can't let our dreams go down the drain. I simply adjusted my goal card to read "I, Peggy McColl, am so happy and grateful that I own a beautiful home where my son, Michel, and I live."

Three months passed, and our house remained unsold. I was at my brother's cottage when I woke up in the middle of the night with the message "Go to the house." This was really bizarre. But I knew exactly what it meant. I didn't understand it. I didn't question it. I still don't know where it came from.

But the next day, with my son and my nephew on board, we drove to the neighborhood where the CHEO home was situated. As we approached the house, I saw a "For Sale" sign on the lawn. I immediately called the real estate agent and booked an appointment to see the house.

When I told some friends I was looking at it again, they said to me, "Why are you going to see that house? You don't have any money. You haven't even sold your old house." I replied, "The real estate agent doesn't know that."

The agent unlocked the door and let me in. I immediately went into the state of imaging how it was already my home. I didn't know how I was going to do it, but I told myself, "This is my home." We walked through the house, and again I felt a very strong sense of ownership. "This is my home," I kept repeating to myself.

Several days later, I asked the real estate agent for a second visit. I brought Michel. We sat at the dining room table, the same dining room table where I had visualized giving thanks for a family dinner, and I said, "Here is what I'd like to offer Dr. John Goodman, the owner of this house. I would like to pay him a respectable amount of money the day I move in. I would like to move in thirty days from now. Then I will pay him an occupancy fee for six months. I will close the deal on December first."

The real estate agent looked at me with a weird expression on his face.

"Is this a legitimate offer?" I asked.

"Yeah, I guess so," he replied, and promised to forward my offer to the owner.

The owner accepted my offer. When that happened, I felt the fear well up. I thought, "Oh, my goodness, what have I done?"

One thing I know about myself is that when I make a commitment to something or someone, I find a way to make it happen.

About a week later, I was having a conversation with a good friend of mine, Val, a successful woman who is totally into personal development. I was telling her what I had done. She pointed out that I had a small amount of money in a retirement account. She advised me to cash it in because a home is an investment. That idea had never occurred to me, and so I called my investment guy; the amount of money, after penalties and fees, was the exact amount I had committed to so that I could move into that new home. The universe was responding to my plea.

I didn't have a lot to pack because the new house was fully furnished and decorated. People I knew who saw the house said, "This is an amazing house. How did you do this?" I didn't tell them I hadn't yet closed the deal because I figured I'd find a way. I had put myself in a position where I had no choice but to follow through.

In that first six months in the house I felt a lot of fear about closing the deal, but I created strategies for switching to emotions that I knew would be far more in keeping with the law of vibration, attracting to me what I wanted. If I felt fear well up, I would start thinking, "Peggy, what is it that you want to experience? I want to experience closing this deal, owning this home. What is it going to feel like when you own the home?" As soon as I asked myself those questions, my breathing changed. I felt more relaxed, and I said to myself, "It's going to feel great. I'm going to feel grateful." Then I connected to what that feels like.

At the time, I was working for a company that had just started selling dedicated World Wide Web access. The company decided to go public. I had absolutely zero experience with initial public offerings (IPOs). I didn't know anything about the stock market, and so I decided to educate myself. I asked a series of questions. I learned that as employees, we would get a really good deal on buying shares, and the day the company went public, we could sell them.

The company was scheduled to go public on October 26; my deal was closing on December 1. Even if it didn't work out, I would have a little time to figure things out. I knew I would.

As we approached October, management realized that they weren't ready, and so they moved the IPO date from October 26 to November 26. My broker told me I would get my money four days later, on November 30. Talk about cutting it close. That had me hyperventilating.

I knew the fear state wasn't going to help me, and so I practiced my switching technique. I put myself back into seeing it all unfold easily and beautifully and harmoniously.

When the company went public, the stock skyrocketed. I sold at its peak on that very day. I got my money on November 30 and took it over to the lawyer's office and closed the deal. The house was mine.

On December 1, I threw a party at the new house I now owned. My son and I lived in that house for almost eight years until I sold it for almost double what I paid.

Going through that experience inspired (and forced) me to create strategies and methods to switch in the face of fear. It caused me to stretch myself. As a result of that experience, I became someone who I wasn't before.

After I told this story at a speaking engagement, an audience member got kind of angry and asked, "Are you telling me that I need to go buy a house without any money?"

"No, that's not what I'm saying," I replied, though that was what he interpreted me to be saying. "I'm saying that one thing I know about myself is that if I make a commitment, I will follow through. That's a certainty I have. If you don't have that certainty about yourself, buying a house without any money is probably not a good idea. But if you know you'll find a way to follow through, you're going to make the decision to follow through."

In the context of this book, this story illustrates that you don't need to know exactly how it's going to be done when you visualize a dream. You just need to commit to doing it. *When you commit to doing it, you will find the way.*

Whatever you are prepared for is what the universe is prepared to give. If you're focused on the good, not just wishing but seeing the good outcome you desire for your business and your success, you've set the stage for positive results.

Most people think the worst, and if that's you, that's what you will attract. When you see the vision of what you want and you feel it, you are in harmony with your goal and will go a long way toward attracting it to you. Have faith and trust that there is a desire out there for what you are bringing forth.

You can have easy goals too, goals you know you're going to achieve or know how you're going to achieve. They won't challenge you the way a stretch goal might, but they won't scare you either. They're still valid and real goals. Getting into the practice of achieving small goals conditions you with confidence to achieve higher goals.

Beware of Scarcity Conditioning

My mother was watching golf on television, and Tiger Woods won the tournament. For some reason, my mother was upset about him winning.

"Why are you mad about that?" I inquired.

"Because Tiger Woods wins all the time."

"What's wrong with that?"

"Because other people can't win," she confessed.

My mother had a scarcity mindset from her upbringing and conditioning. I grew up with that conditioning as well, and so for me to ask for anything that I wanted felt very foreign in the beginning. I had to reprogram myself to step out and say, "Hey, you know what, the universe is ready to respond. Tell the universe what you want." At first that was a really bizarre idea for me to grasp. What is the universe, anyway? The physical universe? No, the universe is a metaphor for unlimited possibilities, for serendipity, for the collective consciousness of humanity.

I remember first hearing many years ago the question "What is it you want?" and thinking to myself, "Maybe I can have only three wishes," kind of like in the Aladdin story. Rub a lamp, and a genie gives you only three wishes. That's another symptom of scarcity conditioning in our culture. It's not like that in real life. You aren't limited. The universe is ready to respond to you. What is it that you truly and deeply want?

Stay Goal-Focused

Because I've become a very goal-focused person, there are certain things I do every single day to keep me moving in the direction I need to be going to achieve my goals.

I consistently list and monitor progress on my activities. These are my daily goal-boosting activities, such as listening to my power life script, doing my affirmations, reading my goal card, watching my vision movie, doing my gratitude exercise, studying positive reading materials, and taking some action, all while measuring and monitoring my levels of faith.

That may sound like a full schedule right there without doing any normal daily work, but you will find, as I did, that your bandwidth of potential expands over time. All these goal boosters can be integrated seamlessly into your life.

Whatever you're prepared to receive is what the universe is prepared to give. As we said earlier, if you're focused on the good, not just wishing but seeing the good you desire for your business, and you know and feel it's really happening, that is the key. Many people think the worst and are plagued by doubt, and more of that is what they end up attracting. When you see a vision of what you want and feel the potential of it, you are in harmony with your goal and will go far in attracting it to you.

The universe was ready for Facebook and social media when it was on the mind of Mark Zuckerberg. Imagine what would have happened if Zuckerberg had been plagued by self-doubt and had been hesitant to launch, wondering if he was ready to bring it forth or if the world was ready for it.

Have faith and trust that there is a desire out there for what you bring forth. Summon the will to animate your vision and goal with concerted action and effort.

Your Success Is Guaranteed

It was Dorothea Brande, the writer and magazine editor, who said, "To guarantee success, act as if it were impossible to fail."

To illustrate how that works in practice, Brian tells the story of a real estate office meeting in 1989. People were struggling. They had dreams of success, but they weren't making sales.

Brian had both huge dreams and huge sales. That gap between dreams and results for the other agents was swallowing them up, sapping their morale. Brian was brought up differently, and he always looked at situations and challenges through rose-colored glasses.

Brian recounts: "I remember blurting out a statement. It just kind of came out of me in this morning meeting with all the other agents. I said to them, 'All I do every day is think about what I can do today to make a deal happen today.' I wasn't worried about the future or whatever. For me, it was always, 'What can I do today to make a deal happen today?' Most people aren't focused like that. They're not thinking. 'What can I do today that's going to get me one step closer to that goal?' But that's what success is about. What can I do today that's going to make a difference in my tomorrow?"

Brian didn't allow himself to get muddled by details. Every day he focused on how to make a deal happen that day. He constantly asked himself, "How can I make this the best possible day it can be to make a difference?"

What does guaranteed success mean? It comes down to faith. What would you do if you knew you could not fail? You wouldn't have trepidation. You wouldn't be frozen in place by doubt. You would have faith in your abilities.

Here are practices and ways of being to keep in mind:

Don't allow yourself to get muddled by details.

Every day, focus on accomplishing something positive that day toward your goal.

Make this the best possible day it can be to make a difference in the life of your business.

Make "My success is absolutely guaranteed" into a mantra you repeat to yourself every day.

What would you do and how would you be if you knew you could not fail?

You won't have trepidation.

You will be fearless.

You will have faith in the outcome.

Get Out of Your Own Way

As a 19-year-old freshman at Southern Illinois University, Sheri Poe was picked up while hitchhiking to work and then held hostage for four hours by a man who violently raped her at gunpoint. When she reported the horrific crime, law enforcement personnel were indifferent—they actually insinuated that she was to blame because she had been hitchhiking—and never brought her assailant to justice.

In an attempt to cope with the trauma and the injustice, along with a slew of health problems she developed as a result of the rape, she threw herself into an intense exercise regimen. During the ensuing decade of high-impact aerobics, she made a discovery that would be the genesis for a successful business idea.

Sheri noticed that there were no workout shoes designed for women and that the men's shoes in her size gave her back pain. There needed to be a workout shoe that would fit a woman's higher arch and narrower heel. She talked with other women at the gym, and they complained of sore backs and aching feet, too, voicing a similar wish for shoes that met their needs.

Working out of their kitchen in a suburb of Boston, Sheri and her husband designed an athletic shoe for women and named it and the company they intended to build around it Ryka. Sheri had worked only as a cosmetics saleswoman; neither of them had experience selling shoes. For the next year they sought funding for the venture, and you can probably guess what happened: they were rejected at every turn.

Finally, a female investment banker Sheri met who was also dedicated to exercise and saw the need for a proper shoe tailored to women opened some funding doors through public stock offerings. She launched her company, and her shoe was carried by Lady Foot Locker in its 588 stores. Sheri achieved her twin goals of operating a profitable business and helping victimized women by dedicating a percentage of Ryka's pretax profits to the ROSE (Regaining One's Self-Esteem) Foundation, a charity she created to help female survivors of violence rebuild their lives.

Sheri's story of success, going from victim to victor, embodies five important principles:

Get out of your own way: To get beyond the emotional trauma of the rape, she summoned a gritty determination and stepped up to fulfill her potential.

A philosophy behind ANY success: She knew clearly what the product need was, had a passion for it, and used the business to make a difference in the quality of people's lives.

Release what holds you back: She found a way to let go of the emotional trauma of her abuse, a scar that could have held her back from business success, by dedicating herself to the mission of helping other similarly abused women.

Drive your financial income with emotional income: Emotional income makes you feel good about what you're doing.

In Sheri's case, that feeling further inflamed her passion for her product, her business, and the impact she was having on others.

Cultivate the law of compensation: You will be compensated in proportion to the good you are delivering to others. For Sheri, this translated into business success and financial independence.

Remember, you are the only one standing in the way of building a successful business and income. Getting out of your own way and surmounting the emotional roadblocks that hold you back involves stepping forward and taking action. That action is the foundational key to all success.

Cultivate a positive mindset.

Develop an awareness of your thoughts and subsequent actions. Reflective meditation every day will help create that awareness.

Pay attention to what you are feeling and thinking in the moment.

Nourish your mind as well as your body each day to heighten your awareness. This is a process that doesn't involve criticism or judgment.

Surround yourself with people who encourage you to be better and do better.

For some lucky people, all this comes naturally; they only have to hone the skills. They were born with it in their DNA or raised to embrace it. My friend Banafsheh Akhlaghi, a constitutional lawyer living in Oakland, California, embodies this.

She emigrated from Iran with her parents when she was a child. Her parents were exceptional, independent-minded people who raised her with the philosophy that your limitations are just the limits of your own thinking.

"If there is a path not paved yet, they will take it," Banafsheh says of her parents. "They don't have fear of rocks in the road." That's the true spirit of the entrepreneur!

After graduating from law school, Banafsheh, at only 27 years of age, became an adjunct professor in constitutional law at John F. Kennedy School of Law. Then the 9/11 attacks took place, and soon thereafter the Patriot Act became law. This turn of events set her off on a path less trodden, one that few others would have the courage to pursue.

A Jordanian man she knew was being questioned by the FBI. She agreed to represent him to obtain a cease and desist order. This case launched her journey as a legal entrepreneur, using the U.S. Constitution to protect the rights of those who were targeted as terrorist suspects only because of their national origin. By 2004, her office had become a nonprofit civil rights organization for people from 24 countries. With that platform, she became a consultant to the United Nations on the reconstruction of a legal system in Iraq.

Being a passionate crusader for causes and being a passionate entrepreneur are both roles that draw upon the same wellspring of individuality, initiative, risk taking, and a visionary call to action. "I learned to listen for the opportunities and the call, to be ready to respond, and to not overthink that response," Banafsheh told me. "We each have a voice within us that cautions, 'You've done this before and it didn't go so well,' or a voice that says, 'You can't accomplish that, so go back.' But we each also have another voice we can nurture. It's the voice that says, 'You are magnificent and brilliant. There isn't anything you can't accomplish. Have no fear.' We have a choice about which voice we allow to guide us."

Make Taking Action a Way of Life

Successful people make a habit of doing things that others don't like to do or won't do. Forming these habits might make us uncomfortable for a while, but relief from that discomfort will come from the energy we dedicate and expend in taking action.

There is no reason why any of us can't have whatever it is that we dream of having as long as we take appropriate action built on a foundation of faith in the outcome.

As a result of making a habit of manifesting what I want in my own life, I realized that I'm the one in control of my emotions. They're like switches, sort of up and down dimmer switches. You're in control of whether they are up or down. It doesn't have to be difficult. You don't have to keep them down and continue to struggle in the face of adversity. You can choose how you respond to situations, and with practice, exercising that choice will become easier for you, as it did for me.

There are natural laws of the universe, and the interactions of human life revolve around them. They are precise laws. We can request something to fulfill a goal, and we can bring that experience into our lives. I think of it as the universe being like a 24/7 truck stop. It's open all the time. We can go out there and make our requests. We can place our orders and have all of them delivered.

We've got the menu of options available to us. That menu is what you would love to experience in your life. What is it you really and truly and deeply want to experience in your life? Make that choice. Set that goal.

If we consider why many people aren't reaching their goals, what do you think the top reasons are? Let's take a look at five of them.

1. Some people think that they're not getting or seeing the results they expect. Very likely, there is a good reason for that. Quite often, it's a very simple reason. Maybe they haven't set any goals to which they are truly committed. They may have desires. They may have wishes. They may express prayers. But they haven't committed to goals without reservation. You've got to do something toward the achievement, and then you've got to believe, put full trust and faith in the outcome.

2. Many times people set a really big goal. They get partway there, but that extra little bit is so tough that they look and think, "God, I've done pretty well," and settle for that half measure and stop. In their minds, they don't think they have given up; they just declare themselves finished. There isn't a goal that is too high. There isn't a goal that is too low. It really comes down to how you are feeling about it and how you *choose* to feel about it.

3. Another reason people don't achieve their goals is that they simply give up. They may get so close that all it takes is another little push, yet they throw up their hands and say, "This isn't working. I'm packing it in. I've had enough." Thus, they don't achieve their goals because they don't see results or see results quickly enough. They don't choose to focus on seeing and feeling what it is that they want to experience. That is hidden by the blinders they choose to put on.

4. They pay too much attention to the negative things other people say about the goal. You need to understand that when you set that big goal, people are going to knock you down. Most people may think you're a little nuts. That's okay. Be aware that it's their negative beliefs they're inflicting on you. You don't have to accept them. If you can find people who will believe in you and inspire you, share the goal with them, but if people are not going to believe in you, don't share it. Keep it to yourself. Again, we come back to choices. It's a choice whether you're going to let somebody's negative opinion of what you're going for affect you. It's so important to recognize that and keep your protective shield of positive thinking in place. What you'll find as you move toward your dreams and become more certain of your direction is that more people will jump on board. Don't expect them to be on board and helping

you in the beginning because that's probably not what you'll experience until you begin to prove their assumptions wrong.

5. Still another reason people set goals and don't reach them is that the goals are not really clear. You have to be specific about what it is that you want. Building a successful business is really a mindset you develop. Develop an awareness of your thoughts and actions. Reflective meditation every day will help create that awareness and add clarity to your goal. It's an important exercise for Brian, whereas I pay attention to what I am feeling and thinking in the moment to help sharpen clarity.

Outcome-Focused Consciousness

On my office desk I keep a symbol of positive manifestation, an Aladdin's lamp. As you may recall, the whole idea behind Aladdin's lamp is that if you rub it, a genie will come out and grant you three wishes.

The universe is like a giant lamp. It's ready to provide any wishes that you may want. The important thing is that you don't have to know how the lamp works.

Make a decision, a goal for your business, and realize you don't have to know exactly how you're going to do it; just set the intention. You're going to find a way if you stay focused on the goal and practice seeing yourself already achieving it. Feel what it is like to have that goal materialize in your life; connect to that vibration alignment, that feeling state.

Good ideas are going to come to you. They're going to hit you when you least expect it. Follow through on them and you'll achieve your goal, probably earlier than you'd planned.

Allow yourself to fall in love with and be deeply inspired by your ideas. Base your goals on those ideas and then take the necessary action. Follow through on those ideas and you will be amazed at how you can create amazing things in your business and in your life that are going to get you where you want to go.

Focus on What You Want, Not What You Don't Want

Inspirational speaker and seminar leader Tony Robbins talks about going to a race car track and being in a vehicle with a professional driver. Tony was in the driver's seat with his trainer beside him, telling him to go faster and faster.

At one point, he was going nearly 200 miles per hour. Tony saw the wall in front of him and started freaking out. He was visualizing what he didn't want to happen, which was to hit the wall. The trainer grabbed Tony's head and turned it toward the curve. The curve was where he wanted him to go, but what Tony was staring at and was fixated on was the wall.

If you're looking at the walls in life, you're going to hit them. If you want to go around the corner safely, you must look toward the corner. Look at what you want, not at what you don't want.

You probably already know what I'm going to say: "You attract to you what you're focused on." You have to change your thinking from preoccupation with the wall to navigating the curves ahead.

Make sure you're summoning joy while you're doing that. People who see you living with joy as you navigate the curves in life with ease will be attracted to you because they will think, "Wow, this person knows what they're talking about. I could learn from this person." Don't let them see fear in you. Let them see you spreading infectious joy.

Goal setting also involves aligning yourself with your desired lifestyle. What is it that you're really looking for? How would you like to live and in what surroundings? What is it that you would like to experience while doing the work that you love?

Achieving business goals is not just about the money; it's about what the money will bring us, the life we'll get to live. We aren't interested in making money just for the sake of making it.

There is a saying: do what you love and the money will follow. But it doesn't always work that way. You have to take action and realize that even slight shifts can lead to major changes.

Create outcome-based mission statements and revenue plans. Ask every day if this is moving you toward or away from your goals. It starts with producing and designing something that other people will want to tell the world about. Carry a goal card. Act as if you'd already accomplished what you set for yourself.

Keep reminding yourself that goals are not for what you'll get but for who you'll become.

Be Specific and Aim High

Whether your goals are personal or business-related, the more specific you are about what you want, the clearer the picture you will have to move toward.

What does a successful business really mean to you? Be very clear on that. Be specific. Is it easily run, not requiring all of your time? Will you still have time for your family? How profitable do you want it to be? How much income do you want? Aim high!

The more specific you are, the more emotionally invested you'll be in your goals. That passion will help drive your success.

It all comes down to being super clear on what it is you really want. Write it down in great detail and post it somewhere obvious where you can't miss seeing it every day. When you have it in front of you all the time, every time you glance at it, you'll think, "What can I do now that's going to get me a little closer to that goal?" It will cause you to do things you wouldn't normally do. That's the purpose. Get emotionally involved and take action.

What can you do right now that's going to get you closer to your goal?

In my business, I set an objective for revenue, for personal income, and for profitability. I'm very accomplishment-oriented.

When I look at the overall goal, when I think about my business and where I see it going and what it's generating in revenue, I break it down into specific numbers.

It's all about intent and a clear vision. How and when you set an intention determines its benefits and results. Many people think these ideas are unorthodox, but Brian and I have seen them at work and have collected the dividends.

It's up to you to become very clear on your intentions and write them down so that you will attract into your life what you envision. This is your opportunity to test-drive these ideas and in so doing show others how they can change their own incomes and lives for the better.

Uncomfortable Goals
and Why They Work

As he was getting ready to go to bed, Bob Proctor turned to his wife and said, "Linda, I know I've got the right goal."

"How do you know?" she asked.

"Because it scares me and excites me at the same time."

When you think about something that you're looking to create, if you've done it before, it's not really a challenge. Bob uses the example of a guy who wanted to buy another Pontiac automobile.

"So, what's your goal?" Bob asked.

"To get a new Pontiac."

"Didn't you buy one four years ago?"

The fellow shrugged and said, "Yeah."

"Then that's not really a goal. You know how to do that. Set a goal that you've never reached before. It's not that you need a better car or anything like that, so set another goal. It's not about what you get with a goal; it's who you become in achieving it."

You need to set goals that make you stretch. If you know exactly how to achieve your goal, it's too easy.

If you can see yourself with your goal, embracing it and experiencing it, you can have it. What you learn through this process is invaluable. These stretch goals stimulate growth and strengthen qualities such as faith, trust, and joy.

If we stop and look fear in the face, we can do that which we think we cannot do. There have been many times, especially with stretch goals, when I've thought about doing or achieving something and felt fearful. I allowed myself to feel the fear, but I went ahead and did it anyway. As a result, what I have experienced in my life has been tremendous success. As author Susan Jeffers wrote, "Feel the fear and go for it anyway."

When you feel overwhelmed, bring yourself back to the mantra "What can I do today that will take me a little closer to that goal?"

Don't worry about the big picture. If you do only one thing, perform one task that will get you a little closer to your goal today. It can be something small and seemingly insignificant. If you take little steps and keep marching forward, in no time at all the uncomfortable stretch goal won't feel quite so overwhelming.

The key is to realize consciously what you're doing to yourself when you are obsessing. When you feel overwhelmed, recognize that fact and acknowledge it and then focus on what you can do today to get you a little closer to that goal. In a matter of days or weeks, that feeling of being overwhelmed will dissipate and you will have a sense of ease.

Take little steps today and focus only on the moment. Whenever you get uncomfortable with something, it's because you're not living in the moment. You're projecting a fear onto the future.

When I start my week and have a very busy schedule, do I feel like doing everything on my daily list? No, certainly not. I get restless just like anybody else. There may be a point in the day when I have a bit of a break in my busy schedule and can walk outside and sit on the patio for a few relaxing minutes. But often I will tell myself that's not what's needed in the moment; it's just a sign of procrastination, and it isn't going to contribute to my business to take this break right now.

Instead I will ask myself, "What if I just make these extra dozen calls to people who are interested in my services and follow through on them? That will move me forward today. It's not going to take me that long to make the calls. I'm going to follow through and make it easy and fun." It's in action that we start to see results.

Goals Must Inspire

You have to be inspired by your goals or you will just be going through the motions and possibly even deluding yourself about what you're accomplishing. Goals must trigger your passion, firm up your dedication, and command your free attention. If you're inspired by your goal, you will experiment and do what's necessary to make it a reality.

A friend of mine once said that when you become comfortable with being uncomfortable, that's when you know you're growing new skill sets. It doesn't mean you always have to be in a state of discomfort. It just means that when you're growing, you're stretching. Sometimes it's a big stretch. Sometimes it's a little stretch. But with each stretch, as happens in yoga, you become a little more flexible.

It's important to keep telling yourself, "I can set the goal, but I don't have to know how I'm going to achieve it. All I know is I *will* achieve it!"

Set Those Stretch Goals

A stretch goal will probably cause you to feel uncomfortable. It's going to excite you and scare you at the same time. If you know exactly how you're going to do it, it isn't a stretch goal. You will learn for certain only when you're experiencing the stretch. A side benefit of being overextended is that you'll also get to know yourself better and be able to gauge the stretch next time.

It's important to note that stretching too far is something that happens far less frequently than not stretching far enough.

Although you may not at this moment believe you're going to get to your goal from where you are, you can grow into that goal. You can begin by turning the negative statement "I don't know how I'm going to get there" into the positive statement "I may not know how, but I know that I will."

Build the muscle of belief so that you feel the accomplishment and see yourself already in possession of that goal.

Personally, I love stretch goals. They enable us to develop and expand personal capacities that will serve us in the future.

For an illustration of how this principle works in practice, let's take a macro goal and reduce it to the micro level.

Brian has committed to working out for an hour every morning on an elliptical machine in his basement. He turns on the TV, jumps on the machine, and gets going. He might have set a goal of an hour, but after 30 minutes he might feel like he is dying. Sometimes you just don't have that full steam in you. He might start thinking of stopping at the 30-minute mark. But he keeps telling himself, "All right, five more minutes." When those five minutes are up, he sets a new small goal of another five minutes. Before he knows it, he has completed the full hour, and he's elated that he didn't quit.

We can apply the same principle to our bigger goals. If you just keep pushing a tiny step at a time, when you finally get to where you want to be, the satisfaction you will get from not quitting is beyond compare.

Taking unfocused action is where most people go wrong, even when they think they're really "working on themselves." I remember receiving an e-mail from a woman who said, "I've been working on this stuff for years. I've been reading the books and going to the seminars, and I get it. I understand it all, but I'm not seeing the results. What's wrong?"

We realized that she was asking the wrong questions. It became very clear to us that she wasn't taking decisive action. She had planned herself and her idea to death.

Polish the Language of Your Goals

When my friend Stephane Morin was 14 years old, his father asked him one night what he wanted for dinner and Stephane casually replied, "A steak." That response angered his father because as a piano player, he never made much money. He had expected his son to request something inexpensive, such as a hot dog.

"We're not lawyers or doctors," Stephane's father yelled. "We'll never be able to afford expensive meals."

Stephane listened, but he refused to believe what his father was saying. It was as if from that moment forward Stephane began inoculating himself against negativity. As Stephane told me, "I vowed right then that when I left home, I would be able to eat steak or lobster whenever I wanted. The philosophy that was to guide my life became clear. How I was going to be in life was going to decide how much money I had."

Part of the philosophy Stephane adopted in pursuing success in his life involves visualizing the completion of his goals after making all those goals very specific: "I was using visualization before I knew what it was and what I was doing. I would get very specific with what I wanted; I chose not to worry about how I would get there. If I wanted a nicer house, I knew that was just an aspect of something bigger. It's really about wanting a defined quality of life. So I defined the quality of life I wanted. How I get to the goal doesn't matter because that comes on its own. The plan changes, but not the goal."

Stephane turned himself into a serial entrepreneur and a self-made man by buying and selling companies. When last I spoke with him, he owned and was president of four companies: a firm in the steel industry, a window and door business, an asbestos decontamination company, and a demolition tool business.

A lot of people get blown way off course by what happens in life. But I put myself in situations where I won't allow myself to fail. I stay sole owner for three or four years of each company that I buy, then I give away up to 30 percent of each company to managers based on how long they stay. That's one way to ensure commitment. People that work in my companies are giving me half of their waking lives in exchange for money each hour. What I do as a manager is teach a way of thinking to my employees—the company is a tool to produce income for everyone contributing inside the company so they can feed their own financial goals.

By having clearly defined and decisive goals, I started seeing opportunities and potential opportunities rather than the obstacles. If I know that banking will be an obstacle to obtaining a company, I throw multiple lines out to eight to twelve bankers. Timing is of the essence. I jump on the opportunities quickly. I do a lot of acquisitions. How do I choose which businesses I buy? It's not by focusing on a specific one. I find the companies by dropping a lot of lines into the water. I always have multiple opportunities that I explore simultaneously. When I buy a business, I feel gratitude but not excitement because the emotional drive belongs in the realization of the goals.

Stephane is someone who embodies the principles for success. He has truly grown the mental foundation of his success by using positive thinking and clarity in defining his goals.

Write down your goals in the present tense and think of them in the present tense. Consider your words as energy in motion. Act and feel as if you were already experiencing the achievement of the goals.

Don't Forget to Have Fun

Inspirational speakers Jerry and Esther Hicks used to travel around the country in a big motor home to all their special events. On the back of their customized motor home was a giant bumper sticker that read "Life is meant to be fun."

Brian and I endorse that sentiment and live it wholeheartedly.

Life is meant to be fun. Making it fun and rendering life easy is a choice you make. Remember that. Repeat it every day. Life is meant to be fun. It's a matter of choice.

Fun is the overlay to commitment. What is it you want? What is it you'd love to experience in your life?

When you're writing down your goal, don't write "I want . . ." because the universe will respond and say indeed you do, meaning that you have the feeling of want. You have to own your goal. Claim it. Integrate it into your thoughts.

What is it that you'd love? If you don't know specifically what you want, don't write anything down because you need to be emotionally excited about the goal you set. We do that through the words that we choose to use and through the message to ourselves and others that we create with confidence.

You can have as many goals as you want. Mark Victor Hansen has described how he would host a New Year's dinner party, but he wouldn't let the guests eat until they wrote out their goals for the next year. You couldn't eat dinner until after you'd written down 101 goals.

It doesn't have to be 101 goals. It can be three goals. Whatever number of goals you set, write them down. Put them on a goal card. Carry it with you. Having fun is really important to me, and so I have that on my goal card. Gratitude is on it as well.

Compose everything in the present tense so that you can truly feel it in your mind and body. Use the present tense as if you were living it right now. It leads you where you want to go in a positive way, not a scary way. Remember that any word that sounds negative will also feel negative.

You've heard the expression "Be careful what you wish for." If you're wishing to eliminate debt, you're focused on a negative, which is what debt is. Turn your language and your thinking around. Commit to emphasizing the positive. Commit to prosperity. Commit to generating new sources of income. If you do that and focus on it, your debt will dissolve.

Your Darn Easy Assignment #1
Congratulate Yourself in Advance

We talk a lot about your future self and who that person might be—who *you* might become—if you take our advice to heart and integrate it into your life today to shape your tomorrow.

Imagine the goals you have set for yourself as if they were already accomplished and you are feeling the elation of your success. Now write a letter to yourself describing what you are feeling with the goals having been achieved. This is a letter you will read again in one year, so write everything in the past tense. Take your time. Put some thought into it.

Now put your letter into an envelope, seal it, stamp it, and address it to yourself, including your full address. Give the letter to someone you trust, a friend or relative, with instructions that it be mailed to you on this date one year hence. Mark that date on a calendar.

What you are doing is subconsciously implanting the thought that you have goals to achieve and a deadline within which to fulfill them. You are also establishing a witness—the person you handed the letter to—who will hold you accountable in the future.

You will be pleasantly surprised by the new energy this little technique can create to keep you motivated and focused on your goal.

Your Darn Easy Assignment #2
Getting Your Goals Straight

Denis and I have an extraordinary life, but I always know it's only going to get better. It's going to get better because I'm taking action. I'm following the principles in this book. This has become a habit and a way of life. Make the practice of feeling your goals as normal as breathing. Have this be a way of life.

Part of nurturing our spirits, our lives, and our goals is taking action every single day toward the achievement of those goals. That means making a commitment. Feel as if all these goals that you've set for yourself are already reality. Walk around with a smile on your face. Drive down the highway of life with a smile of achievement on your face.

This is a fun assignment. It involves evaluating your goals. Take a look at the goals you've written down. If you haven't done that yet, do so. Write them in your own hand.

There is a really interesting connection that occurs when you take a pen to paper or to your goal card and simply write your goals down. It amplifies the vibration of the energy of the goals.

You can type them out, too. Keep the goal cards in view. Give thanks for them as well, as if they have already been accomplished, because gratitude is such an important ingredient for success.

A Sample Tracking Sheet

This Week I Am Committed To:

ACTIVITY	MONDAY	TUESDAY	WEDNESDAY	THURSDAY	FRIDAY	SATURDAY	SUNDAY
Write in my gratitude journal each day							
Listen to my power life script							
Watch my manifestation movie							
Meditate 2 × 20 mins							
Read affirmations with enthusiasm							
Feel, believe, know with absolute faith							
Read my goal card 10x a day							

On a scale of 1 to 5, how would you rate yourself on completing these goal-achieving activities each day?

   5: outstanding

   4: as expected

   3: average

   2: could have used more effort

   1: almost no effort

PART III

A Practical Approach for Success with Ease

Your word is your wand. The words you speak create your own destiny.

—FLORENCE SCOVEL SHINN

Movement Toward Success

Is what you're doing now helping you become who you want to be in the future? Little steps taken one at a time will get you where you need to go. You don't need to know the whole path for getting there. Take some kind of action, and the next steps will appear. Move your idea forward with simple steps at first. Learn the difference between doing to be busy and moving forward toward a goal. Condition yourself to align actions with goals.

The Order of Things

Whatever your passion is, decide how you can monetize it. There isn't always a particular order. Ask yourself what is most important to you right now. Understand what is required to get the results you are looking for. When you have a clear vision of what you want, the order of steps will manifest itself.

Embrace Imperfect Action

Imperfect action means you step out and start doing instead of plodding. Imperfect action can force you to commit to a path that pays off. You don't need to know how to do everything. Do the best with what you have. Imperfect action is better than no action at all.

Accountability Expands Your Chances for Success

First, learn to hold yourself accountable for keeping your word and meeting your goals. Find accountability partners. Become accountable to one another on the progress of your businesses and your lives. You will become more consciously aware and focused on the end result. Pick someone to be accountable to. The likelihood of actually following through and taking care of those tasks is much higher if you have others holding you accountable to your word. It's a simple thing that can make a big difference.

Find the Good in Adversity and in People

Draw to you the kind of people who want to do business with you. Always look for the good in people. Find something to be grateful for and focus on that. Leave everyone you come into contact with better off because of that contact and in the fact that they met you. When things don't go the way you want in your business, don't let doubt undermine your spirits. Look for the good in what you have and what you are doing. That will raise your confidence level. There is a gift in every adversity.

Release What Holds You Back

If you are struggling and something bothers you, if you focus on it, it will attract more of the same. Find a way to let it go. Know where to go to get help to release the negative. Everyone confronts emotional challenges that can undermine his or her business. Negativity is contagious. Half the success battle is awareness of what is really bringing you down.

Put Tools in Your Toolbox

What are the resources or habits you have for success? What keeps you focused on having a positive mindset? These are skill sets you have and may not be consciously using with regularity. Do a self-assessment of your tools. Keep a daily goal list. Make people feel special. Regularly measure your results. You must regularly use your toolbox to get the benefits.

Building Networks, Influences, and Teams

Relationships are the key to success in business. The more help you give others, the more they will want to help you. Reach out. Stay in touch. Create a relay team. Strive to surround yourself with people who are contributors to this world. The members of your network will want to introduce you to their networks as well. Your mentors should be results-oriented trailblazers. Who is helping you with your vision? Your team is a reflection of your organization. Who you hang out with is a reflection of who you are. Surround yourself with supportive, like-minded people. Be confident but also be humble and people will want to work with you.

Your Darn Easy Assignment #1: Make Yourself Accountable

Your Darn Easy Assignment #2: Focus on Your Outcomes

Movement Toward Success

When my friend Phil Nguyen's parents separated, he became an angry teenager with no positive direction in life. Fortunately for him and for society, he took up a martial arts practice that saved his life.

"I started doing push-ups instead of pushing drugs," he told me. "I started punching into shields rather than punching into walls." Martial arts gave him focus, discipline, and respect. It also taught him how best to direct his energy so that it wasn't unfocused or squandered.

After 27 years of training, he received a seventh-degree black belt in tae kwon do in April 2012, becoming Master Phil, and made a decision to share his pride and joy at this accomplishment by posting on Facebook for the first time. He expressed thanks and joy to everyone who had helped him on his journey and forgiveness to everyone who had hurt or hindered him.

That first post on Facebook set in motion the idea for a challenge he presented to himself that would in short order lead to a whole new level of recognition and success.

"I challenged myself to write one Facebook post a day for the next 100 days. By day 7, this had reignited my passion for writing. I realized that I had the discipline to post every day. At about day 85, a friend sent me an e-mail, inviting me to be a guest columnist for a newspaper with 169,000 readers a day."

This 100-day challenge gave him awareness of what he now calls the 1 Percent Rule: mastery comes from putting out 1 percent every day for 100 days.

Soon thereafter, Master Phil wrote a book, *Black Belt Leadership: 9-Point Path to Wisdom, Inspiration, and Enlightenment*. The business he owned, the Black Belt Excellence Martial Arts Academy, attracted flocks of new students. He began doing training programs for corporate employees and the Royal Canadian Mounted Police.

"Although I'm a black belt in martial arts, really, I teach people how to become black belts in life and business. Martial arts practice translates into business success by offering you the development of a focus on serving your clients with high-value solutions, by giving you the discipline to go in and through challenges to achieve success, and by the respect you show for yourself and for your customers and their needs."

"Seek not to improve yourself 100 percent in one day," advises Master Phil. "Seek to improve yourself 1 percent per day for 100 days. That is the true path of self-mastery."

Here is Master Phil's challenge to you for the 1 Percent Rule of Daily Discipline:

Every hour, do something good.
Every day, learn something new.
Every week, connect with someone inspiring.

Every month, create something beautiful.
Every year, achieve something great.
Every decade, reinvent yourself proactively.
Every moment, realize your life is a miracle.

Take Little Steps Toward Your Goal

Some years ago I had a conversation with someone who had set a goal of climbing Mount Kilimanjaro, which is a pretty ambitious and aggressive goal for anyone. We were talking about how you don't always know what you're going to be up against no matter how much you plan. If you are a mountain climber, you don't know with certainty what kind of terrain you will face because weather changes the terrain. You prepare for it as best you can, but what often happens is that you have a totally different experience as you're moving along to the top.

It's a similar situation when we're working toward our goals and we set a plan and start moving in that direction. Quite often, we don't know what the terrain is going to look like, what we're going to be up against, how we're going to feel, or what we really need to get to the next level.

In those uncertain circumstances, I'll sometimes create a longer-range business plan. By longer range, I mean a year, which is probably the farthest out that I'll be thinking. If someone tells me that he or she has a program that's going to help me map out the next 5 or 10 years, I'm not attracted to that. I'm more of a short-term planner, because that enables me to make greater, grander, and bigger plans as a result of the flexibility I can bring to bear. I can take advantage of unforeseen opportunities.

Little steps will take you where you need to go. You don't need to know the whole path. Take some kind of action, and the next steps will appear. Move your idea forward with simple steps.

Here is a great question for contemplation: "Is what you're doing now helping you become what you want to be in the future?"

We're given this gift of life, this wonderful opportunity to do what we love and have it be easy and fun. When you ask questions like this one, do you really contemplate what you're doing now, or do you automatically compare yourself with others and what they have accomplished? Or do you start comparing yourself with other people who are struggling and not making it and worry whether you will end up like them?

If you're doing things today that are going to improve your life in the future, tomorrow, next week, whatever it may be, as long as you're focused on that, you will never be like the people you don't want to become. They're not worried about their future. They're not taking appropriate action or any action at all. That is virtually always the case. Get away from comparing yourself with others.

Just do what you can do today that will make a difference tomorrow.

Be aware of what you're thinking. Notice what you're saying. Observe how you're comparing yourself with others if indeed you are comparing. What this process does is put you in a mindset of competitiveness.

Make a List of What Needs to Be Done

To keep momentum behind movement toward success, one thing that I do is create what I call a working plan or a working document. It's not anything formal. It's a spreadsheet mapping out what needs to be done over a period of time.

As I move into each week, I identify what I will do that week that I'm committed to and that will take me forward. Each item on the list must take all my projects and revenue production in a forward direction.

It's not about overanalyzing. It's just a list that is based on a conscious decision about what I am very much aware of. I ask myself, "Is this contributing to my business, or is it taking away? Is this item taking me closer to my goals, or is it taking me farther away from achieving them?"

If it's taking me closer, I'm going to do it. If it's taking me farther away, I won't do it. This is a simple technique of prioritizing what's most important each week to keep your momentum going in the right direction.

Condition Yourself

Over time, continually taking action to move toward your goal will condition you to think this way habitually. As a result, you will find your actions will be in alignment with that thought process because that's where action comes from. It is triggered by the willpower of your conscious mind, or through repetition it is engraved in your subconscious.

In my case, the woman who shows up for work is also the wife, the mother, and the grandmother. These are the various roles that I play in my life. Thus, when I'm talking about setting outcomes or goals and continually moving toward them, it encompasses all the aspects of my life. It involves my relationship with my husband and what we have together and what we do, and it involves my son and my grandson as well.

Take all the elements of your life into consideration when you set your goals and establish these weekly priorities. It's a holistic approach. It also requires flexibility because the various elements of your life will be changing. Your relationships may change. Even your ultimate goal may undergo a transformation.

When I started my company, people told me I needed to create a detailed business plan, and so I went to business school and learned how to create such a plan. Twenty years ago, I wrote the business plan for my business when I incorporated it. I think I found it in a box the last time we moved. I probably tossed it. It put a big smile on my face because I realized that it was really the only time that I created a long, detailed business plan.

If I had adhered to that business plan, my company never would have thrived because I would have lost the flexibility to navigate all the unpredictable changes that occurred in my business and in my life.

Now I keep it really simple. The goal is always specific and concrete, but the plan on how to get there is flexible and changing.

That's what we're all about—simple, easy, and focused. Set objectives and move toward them by ensuring that you're doing whatever is taking you closer to achieving your goals.

The Order of Things

In pursuing your plan and your goal, there isn't always a particular order in which to do things. Ask yourself what's most important to you right now. Understand what is required to get the results you are looking for. When you have a clear vision of what you want, the order of steps will usually be manifest.

Whatever your passion is, decide how you can monetize it. For instance, in today's business world we all know that everyone needs a website. How can you drive traffic to your website? You need a database of names and e-mail addresses. Those are the fundamentals. That's part of the order of things, and it probably needs to come relatively early in your process.

Some people may work really well with long-term plans and a particular order. Brian and I like short-term plans because we find that if you are really leaping and growing and stepping out and doing some crazy cool things, three months from now you can be in a completely different place.

If you plan out five years from now, you may be such a different person or find yourself in such different circumstances that the original plan won't be relevant anymore. If you're working every day and really focusing on the different things you're doing, you will get results that nobody else is getting. Three months from now, you may be creating something different because you and your business are different.

We can't emphasize this enough: you don't need to know how or exactly what you need to do to get to where you're going. You just need to know where you intend to end up.

Brian and I start moving in the directions we've set for our respective businesses, and we adjust as we go along. A goal isn't something you do once and then you're done with it. It's something that becomes a habit pattern for you as you set new goals and replicate your success.

We're habitual creatures. When you get into the habit of setting and achieving goals, you gain momentum. Once you achieve a goal, you're working on the next one. You find that you're constantly expanding, evolving, and growing.

Set High-Revenue Goals

When I'm setting outcomes for my business, I'll set a high-revenue goal. That's where I start with any plan. It doesn't matter when in the year I do it. We could start today even though part of the year has already gone by.

When you set an outcome, let it start with these questions: "What would you love to have and where would you love to be? What would you love to create? How much money do you want that creation to generate?"

When I go through my revenue goal process, I start by setting the intention. Then I start thinking about the three questions that I incorporate in my process:

1. Where is there a need or want in the marketplace?
2. What can I deliver on?
3. What will people pay for or invest in?

As I start to think of revenue sources, I recall what I've done in the past that's been really successful. I think of what I'm doing today that is really working, and then I factor in how I can serve people even better. My mindset of planning comes from a place of service. How can I bring greater value to those I'm very blessed to already serve? Then I brainstorm what those revenue sources could be to meet the goal.

As a businesswoman who has seen my business grow over several decades, I recognize that at the end of the year, what I'm always looking for is profit. I want a profitable business because if it's not profitable, obviously I will quickly be out of business. Therefore, I create a revenue plan that involves profitable new activities or new twists on already profitable activities. I'll outline everything that could be a revenue source. These could be things that I'm doing, things that I've done, and things that I'm planning on doing. Taken together, they need to produce the revenue goal I've set.

Here is what wonderfully happens every time in my experience. Let's use some round numbers to make this easier to explain. Let's say the revenue goal is $20 million. I write out or put in a Word file or Excel spreadsheet everything that is a possible revenue source. Ultimately, what I end up with is a revenue forecast that is greater than the goal. These could even be made-up numbers. Quite often, that's where all of your projections start—in your imagination.

The late Neville Goddard, an inspirational teacher and author, taught us to think from the goal. He said that if you set an outcome to generate $20 million in your business, you must already be thinking like a businessperson who is generating $20 million from that business. Even though you may not know how you're going to generate the $20 million, if you see yourself doing it and feel and believe you are already a businessperson who is generating $20 million, and if you are committed to thinking from that place, useful ideas are going to come to you. You will generate valuable ideas to make that revenue goal a reality.

This is one more quality that clearly differentiates successful people from unsuccessful people. You must be willing to take action without knowing all the steps involved. You must be willing and able to take that action with full faith in yourself and in the outcome you seek. Once this thought process becomes a habit, your revenue goals will fall into place more easily than your previous self ever imagined possible.

Embrace Imperfect Action

Rather than plodding along and being cautious to a fault, taking imperfect action involves stepping out of your comfort zone and doing something without really knowing all the steps that will get you where you want to go. Sometimes the biggest achievements in life are accomplished by leaping with faith and trusting that the next step will become clear once you take the first one. Imperfect action is better than no action at all.

To give you a good example of how that works, Brian started a business that required a computer and an e-mail address, and so he bought a computer, got an e-mail address, and started learning on his own. He started sending e-mails out to clients and prospective clients. He didn't have a clue what he was doing. It was imperfect action to be sure, but he stepped out and took action. Even if it was not done with the best form, it was better than doing nothing at all. He tested out his idea and perfected it by trial and error. That imperfect action forced him to commit to a path that has paid off for him.

Do the best with what you have and trust that other experts will perfect what you are doing. You don't need to know how to do everything.

When I reflect on my decision to write my first book, I realize that I didn't let the fact that I made it only through high school hold me back. If I had thought I needed to have a degree in journalism or creative writing, it would have stopped me from taking any action.

At the end of the day, you can plug the holes until you have a completed project. Then you can bring on the best people who can take it to the next level.

I've seen so many people who have great ideas and allow those ideas to die with them. It's like that old expression "Don't die with your music still in you." Release the music of your ideas. Take some action, even imperfect action, so that the music doesn't die.

Accountability Expands Your Chances for Success

Find yourself some accountability partners.

Once you have picked someone to be accountable to, your likelihood of actually following through and taking care of those tasks is so much higher.

A study at Brigham Young University showed that when people say, "Wow, that is a really good idea," there is a 10 percent chance they will actually take action to accomplish it. That goes up to 25 percent if they make a vow: "I'll do it." The chances of success go up to 40 percent if they create a plan to accomplish the goal. What takes the probability of action from 50 percent to 95 percent is when they commit to someone else that they will accomplish the goal and share their progress with that person on a regular basis.

Wouldn't you rather be in the 95 percent bracket with your idea and your follow-through? It's such a simple thing that can make a tremendous difference, yet it's so often overlooked.

Brian and I both have accountability partners, and we are also accountable to each other to progress in our businesses and in our lives. Every Monday, we send each other a list of what we will accomplish that week, and we support each other in achieving that. At the end of the week we give each other a synopsis of how it all went. It makes us more consciously aware and focused on the end result. When you do it regularly, it becomes a part of the way you do business and run your life.

Another accountability partner is a very close friend, Arielle Ford. We've been doing this every week for years.

What do I mean by holding each other accountable? At the beginning of the week, we e-mail each other. I'll send her an e-mail describing how this week I will easily, joyfully, harmoniously, and for the good of all concerned accomplish all these items and more. I'll list the items: everything that I know will be contributing toward the goals and objectives that I set for myself. They are mostly business-related, but there will be some items that are of a personal nature. Then I express what I am grateful for.

There is no judgment about the task list or its completion. If I send an e-mail to Arielle, she often will send back a reply saying, "Yes, indeed you did this," or "Yes, you will do this," or she will give her congratulations. We exchange a spirit of support and positivity. We often inspire each other. I'll see that she set an objective, and I'll say, "Oh, yeah! That's a really good one. I think I'm going to add that one to mine."

We'll check in with each other midweek. "How are you doing with your list? I've crossed this off mine. I've added a couple more items." At the end of the week, we provide each other with an update. What did we actually accomplish? Again, no judgment is expressed.

Our process isn't complicated. It's a support system. It helps us keep our goals clear and our priorities straight. And it works as advertised!

Find the Good in Adversity and in People

The first time Brian and his father organized a seminar cruise, it went really well. They filled the whole ship. When they were not in the seminars, the participants had fun visiting some of the islands along the way and sightseeing.

Brian and his father wanted to repeat their success, and so they booked the ship again, but this time several unexpected things happened. The recession hit, and they didn't sell out the ship. They were charged an extra fee for every empty room and lost a lot of money on that cruise.

Brian's father was sharing this situation with Michael Beckwith, who was on the cruise, and Beckwith made a memorable statement in response: "Harvest the good, forgive the rest."

You can take that statement as a healing balm for anything that is negative and is adversely affecting you. Take whatever happened and harvest the good from it. Whatever you can learn from it, harvest the good. Forgive the rest. Any of the negative experiences that have affected you or hurt you, whatever the negative effect may be and however deep the wound goes, do your best to let them go.

Surround Yourself with the Right People

A big contributor to any success is surrounding yourself with really good, trustworthy people who are going to inspire you to do more with your business, to give more, and to be more as a person. Bounce ideas off them and brainstorm with them. A couple of good minds working with you can take your idea and make it even bigger. You can take your business to a whole new level.

Another really important practice is always to speak good about the people with whom you work or interact socially. What you say about others tends to get around even when you think you're speaking in confidence. Never share negative things. We've all got negative thoughts about others that we want to share, but there is no point focusing on that. Spreading negativity only comes back to haunt us.

One of the things I learned as a kid was that you should make the person you're speaking to feel special, as if that person has the letters MMFI—Make Me Feel Important—written on his or her forehead. You do that by being totally in the moment. You're not thinking about what happened yesterday or what you need to do later in the day. You're focused on the here and now on this human being in front of you and the interaction the two of you are having. Seek to leave everyone you have contact with better off in some way because of that contact.

Brian's dad makes people feel special all the time. At every one of his events, you will find him complimenting many of the people in the room. He does it genuinely and with all the sincerity in the world, and people appreciate being on the receiving end.

There is always something good—and accurate—you can find to say about almost anybody if you try. Once you start finding and appreciating qualities in others and voice that appreciation, you will find your relationships will improve and your business will grow. People will want to work with you. I can't tell you the volume of e-mails I receive from people who want to work with me. It's a really nice feeling. I know I have a great reputation out in the Internet marketing world, and it's entirely because I try to make all the people I deal with feel like they are the most important people in the world.

Harold Kushner once wrote, "If you concentrate on finding whatever is good in every situation, you will discover that your life will suddenly be filled with gratitude, a feeling that nurtures the soul."

If you concentrate on finding whatever is good and positive in every situation, no matter what it is, you will begin to transcend the adversity. Whether you're experiencing challenges or facing something that's scaring you or upsetting you, ask yourself what the good is in that situation. Maybe what you are learning about yourself is the lesson you will take away from it. Whatever it is you find that is good, feel and express gratitude for it. When we get into a spirit and feeling of gratitude, it nurtures the soul and opens us up for more of the good to come into our lives.

When things don't go the way you want in your business, don't let the doubts that may surface undermine your spirits. Look for the good in what you have and what you are doing. It may take a shift in thinking to see what is good about the situation or the experience, but that will raise your confidence level. If you lose a client, the good may not be apparent immediately, but find the good in seeking new clients and new opportunities. Keep reassuring your inner self that there is a gift to be found in every adversity. Make it a mantra.

If you're always focused on the good in situations and other people, it puts you in an optimistic and generous state of mind. All it takes to master that is a little bit of practice. One thing I love doing is firing off an e-mail to somebody just when I'm thinking about that person. I'll send an e-mail saying something as simple as "I'm thinking of you. You're a wonderful person. I love working with you."

Just keep sending those good vibes out there. Stay focused on the good. When you touch other people's lives with notes of thanks or support, it will make them feel better and they will remember your thoughtfulness. You make lasting impressions that way. It will also make you feel better about yourself and your life and shift you into a completely different state of mind. If you practice doing things like that every day, your whole life really does become better, and that pays incalculable dividends to your business.

Release What Holds You Back

If you are struggling and you focus on that, it will attract more of the same. That's a truism. It's no different in business. If you focus on the setbacks, you invite more of the same.

Find a way to let go of the negativity. Release it. Know where to go to get help if you need it to release the negative. Everyone confronts emotional challenges, and the negative repercussions of the feelings generated can undermine your business if you aren't careful. Negativity is contagious. But so is optimism.

Half the battle is having awareness of what's bringing you down. Ask yourself what else this situation could mean. Maybe the other person is going through a tough time right now. Don't take ownership of someone else's negativity. Are you allowing negativity to overburden you? What would expressing love (for yourself or others) do now? It will shift your thinking.

If you're looking to create greater success in your life, it's essential to be flexible. Brian is a good example of someone who doesn't hold on to upset, anger, or resentment. That's a really healthy way to be.

We all experience challenging times. That's a given. There will always be cycles to everything in our businesses and our lives. Ideally, we have a lot more up times than down times, but we all know there will be challenging times. The key is to realize that it's temporary and to avoid fixating on it. Just do whatever you can to correct it with the faith that better days are just around the corner.

When something in your business isn't going right, take a step back and ask why. Who can you brainstorm with and share some of your issues with who can potentially help you? Rather than just sitting at home and stewing over it or crawling under the covers, get out there and actively try to change the situation. Usually the best way is to find other people who can help you see the lay of the land from a completely different angle. That can change things for you. It's probably less involved than you think it is. It's about acknowledging the problems and finding solutions for them.

If you hang on to resentments and other emotional baggage, it becomes a cancer. If you learn how to take a lighthearted or transcendent view of challenging situations, you open yourself up to more good. There are people out there who would love to help you. Allow yourself to express that need and embrace what others have to offer you.

Put Tools in Your Toolbox

Denis and I met a man named Ian who operates a pool installation company. We were putting a pool in our backyard, and Ian was helping us decide what we really wanted.

At one point in our discussion, I said, "Ian, I really appreciate you." He turned and looked at me as if I had two heads and replied, "I can't tell you how rare it is for a customer or a prospective customer to say they appreciate me."

Here is a guy in a service business. He's devoting time to consider what our needs are and provide a price quotation with the potential of getting our business. He made us feel as if we were with a friend acting as a consultant instead of with a stranger trying to sell us something.

As soon as Ian left, Denis and I told each other how much we liked him. His whole approach had been service-oriented. We wanted to give him our business. I already had the checkbook out, and I didn't care what the quote was going to be. I knew I was going to do business with him because he treated us with respect. He showed that he really cared. He embodied the qualities of the type of person I want to surround myself with.

What Ian possesses, whether he knows it or not, is a skill set, a personality tool in his business toolbox that serves him well in connecting with people and as a result generating new business and a greater income potential.

What are the personal resources or habits you have cultivated for success? What keeps you focused on being in a positive and caring state of mind when you are dealing with clients, customers, and business associates? These are skill sets you may already have and may not be using consciously, effectively, or with enough regularity.

Create Mood Pick-Me-Ups

One tool I use regularly to put me in a good emotional state for business interactions is a gratitude journal. The goal card that I refer to frequently is another tool to keep me goal-focused.

Perhaps the most powerful tool I use is my power life script, a description of my life, written in the present tense, using positive words to detail what my life will look like when I have achieved my goals. It's recorded, 25 minutes long, and I listen to it every day. This is what I refer to as one-touch enlightenment because I just touch the play button.

You can customize a meditation or power life script by going to relaxwithbob.com. There you can create a motivational tool to keep you in the right mindset for achievement. This is more effective than most self-help books.

You must use your toolbox with regularity to get the most benefits.

Keep a Daily Goal List

When you are executing the steps in your goal plan, you may get distracted and bogged down when a lot is happening, particularly if you're someone who likes to keep track of everything in your head.

In my case, I always take a pad of paper and set it right beside my computer; every night before I go to bed, I write down the top five or six things I want to accomplish the next day. It could be people I need to talk to, a project I need to complete, whatever the necessary tasks may be.

When morning comes, I jump in and hammer away at the list until it is done. I'm a morning person, and so I get up super early and go through that list one point at a time. If you take focused action on achieving something today that is going to make a difference for you tomorrow, you will never look back and your future is going to be phenomenal. I'm living an amazing life, and it's because every day I'm taking action toward something to make it better. It's as simple as that.

Stay in Touch with Your Clients as Much as You Can

Do it in a positive way. Keep your name in front of them, speak highly of them with everybody you deal with, and treat everybody well. Then take actionable steps every day that will take your business one step farther. That is in alignment with always giving the impression of increase. It's having people feel like their lives are greater, grander, and increased in a positive way just from interacting with you and being in your presence.

They say little things make a big difference. These are some of the things that can make the biggest difference in your life. Not just in your business life but in your personal life, too. If you genuinely care about people and stay in constant touch with them, you will be the first person they think of when your product or services are needed.

Go to Industry Events

Don't show up at industry events and sit on the sidelines without participating. Show up and fully participate, interact with others, and embrace the program.

Circulate widely, be fully present, and talk to and listen to people, treating them the way you want to be treated—with attentive respect. You will make new connections that could end up benefiting your business in ways you cannot imagine.

Regularly Measure Your Results

This is just a matter of noticing and recording. When we're measuring results, we set objectives for ourselves and keep our attention on the progress we make.

When we're looking at our business, we never lose sight that it is numbers-based. Besides revenue-based profitability, there are many ways to measure your results.

Sometimes the measure is the number of clients in certain programs. Sometimes it's increasing your database by a certain number. Sometimes it's the number of affiliates or partners that are promoting whatever it is that you're doing or partners helping you deliver something. Whatever yardsticks you use, they're usually numbers-based. It could even be just paying attention to how your customers are responding and their level of happiness with your product or service.

My friend Diane Craig, who runs the company Corporate Class Inc., once sent out a survey to everyone on her database that she was a little nervous about. I was a recipient of her survey, which basically asked what I thought of her. What is my impression of Diane Craig? What do I think of her performance? What are her strengths? What are the areas in which I think she could improve? This was a measurement process. Why did she do it?

She did it because Diane Craig, who is a very successful businesswoman, is all about bringing greater value. It felt risky for her to make that request of people who know her, some of whom know her only a little. She did it anyway because she knew the information this risk generated would contribute to her continued success.

When you're measuring your results, keep it simple. Notice where you are compared with your projections. If you set an objective to get to a certain place and you're not there yet, this is an opportunity to evaluate whether you need to find another way. Maybe the approach you're taking isn't working. Maybe you need to adjust your strategy, build your e-mail list, and work on your brand. One of the best things you can do for your business, especially if you're in an online business, is to build your prospect base. The wider your reach, the stronger your client relationships, which will become a solid foundation for your business.

It's really foundational; it's not something that starts and stops. Your job isn't done once you've built the foundation. You must continue to nurture and maintain it. Ask yourself, "Is the foundation cracking? Do I need to strengthen it in another area?" A foundation is only as stable as its maintenance.

Brian is constantly monitoring how many subscribers he has. If he detects a drop in the numbers, he immediately looks into why. He is always asking questions and looking for ways to generate new subscribers who will receive his message. If he is doing an online offer, he's looking at how many people are clicking on that offer. If he's getting lots of clicks, great! He still asks what it is that's causing that response. If he's not generating the traffic he wants, he explores what might be causing that. Then he tweaks everything to see if this will help pick up the pace. Many people don't do these periodic measurements, yet it's so important.

It's also important always to monitor your business. How is it going? What can I do to make it a little better? Always try to think and get outside of the box. Don't allow yourself to get stuck in the rut of a regular daily routine that lulls you into a state of complacency. There are always new ways to make your business grow. Experiment!

Learn to Manage Through Challenging Times

We invite you to commit to having your life go well all the time. Is that realistic?

The word *realistic* should be removed from our vocabulary. Maybe we can create a new definition. What does realism really mean? Is it realistic to have your life go well all the time?

On the basis of my experience, I really do believe that it is realistic. My life does go well most of the time. Maybe not all the time, but I'm committed to having it go well all the time. Mental preparation is the key.

As a former pilot, Denis is definitely one to talk about the importance of preparation. He went for pilot training and test flights many times throughout the year just to keep his skills sharp. Being in simulators was a regular occurrence. They would simulate an engine falling off the plane or a bird strike. If pilots are prepared for these sorts of occurrences, they will overcome those challenging times more easily if and when they come up.

Preparation of this kind is what I call a skill in the toolbox of effective strategies.

How do you foretell when a challenge is on the horizon? How do you know when to open your toolbox?

Sometimes you may not know; it may creep up on you or jump out of the shadows. But generally speaking, there are usually indicators if you pay attention and open up to awareness.

Awareness is an important skill to have if your life is going to be darn easy. You can anticipate many looming challenges by paying close attention to your gut instinct. The more you use your intuition, the more you will learn to trust it.

Observation will help inform your intuition. Notice if you're having some challenges with your customers. What is it that they want more of? What are their issues that even they don't understand? A lot of this is nonverbal; they may never tell you, but your powers of observation and intuition can prompt you to be proactive.

Pay attention to your clients, to your prospects, and to yourself and your own feelings. Tap into how you're feeling about certain people and situations for clues about what needs fixing. Those intuited insights will provide you with good indicators of whether you will need course corrections as you're going along.

All these tools are techniques that Brian and I successfully use. We invite you to implement them. It's not just a matter of collecting tools in your toolbox and having them gather dust. It's a matter of pulling out and utilizing what you need when you need it. Reassure yourself that when challenges arise, you are well equipped to deal with them.

Building Networks,
Influences, and Teams

B rian has a real estate background. He was always in the top percentage for the real estate firm RE/MAX International. Why
he was a success seemed so simple to him that he never understood
why everybody else wasn't successful, too. He realized that much of
his success came down to maintaining a simple list of names.

He would send out a letter to all his past clients and all his
prospects once a month. This was before e-mail. He would give
information of possible interest and value: the state of the market,
a list of great mortgage brokers who could provide better rates than
the bank, and so on. It didn't matter what the letter contained; it
was a reason for Brian to stay in touch with his clients and prospects.

Every time he sent out letters, he would always get a number of
listings and new buyers that would generate sales. It was that easy.
What always amazed Brian was that very few agents he knew did
that. Most agents would sell someone a house and never reach out
to the client again.

Here's what Brian and I take from this example: No matter what
kind of business you're in, there is a reason to stay in touch with your

current clients, your past clients, and your future prospects. That contact translates into revenue for your business.

When e-mail came along, Brian expanded the contacts he had maintained via snail mail. At first, he had only about 300 e-mail addresses. He e-mailed those people a simple inspirational quote from Monday to Thursday and an uplifting story every Friday. That was it. This technique worked wonders for his business.

Keep Your Name in Front of Your Clients

It doesn't matter what you do. There should be something that you can send your clients, past clients, and prospective clients. You don't have to do it daily. You can do it once a week.

You need to send people something that is going to keep your name in front of them and in their thoughts. They might not do anything with it immediately, but a year down the road they might, whether they are purchasing a service or a product from you. That would be a sale that never would have happened if you had not stayed in touch with them.

After Brian established his habit of staying in touch with his clients, he quickly got good responses, and he noticed that his list was growing. People would forward his e-mail to others, and they would sign up as a result. Then Brian offered a $30 product for sale. It was a simple book and CD to test the waters, so to speak. He immediately got sales; that was when he really knew he was on to something with huge potential.

Over the last decade or so, Brian's list has grown into a few hundred thousand names, and it earns millions of dollars a year. It was darn easy.

Even if you start with only 10 people, it doesn't matter. Whether they are clients, prospects, friends, or whatever category they fall into, make a decision to send them an e-mail at least once a week. Include with it something useful, humorous, inspirational—whatever brings some value to their day. Make sure it's related to what it is that you're doing. Keep it in harmony with yourself. Keep it short and simple. Long newsletters never get read. At the bottom of your e-mails, make sure you have your name, your service, your company, and whatever it is you're selling or promoting. If you're not selling or promoting anything right now, just keep your name in front of them.

If you're going to e-mail just once a week, make it a Tuesday, Wednesday, or Thursday. Never e-mail on a Monday. Whatever you do, do it consistently. This will establish trust over time, and this consistency will generate results.

It's an unbelievable way to build any kind of business. Whether you are a Subway sandwich franchise owner or a major Internet marketer, anyone can derive benefits from staying in touch with customers on a regular basis.

This is one of our most effective methods for success. There are some very simple software solutions available that will enable you to stay in touch with the people with whom you do business.

Your Relationships Are the Key to Success in Business

Who do you know and why? These are important questions in determining the right formula for your success.

Brian's main focus most days is staying in touch with people and asking them, "What can I do for you?" The more help you provide others, the more they will want to help you. That's another one of the truisms we keep repeating.

Reach out. Stay in touch. It can be an e-mail, but personal contact and phone calls are best. If you can do it with those who have influence in your industry, that's even better. Focus outward first. That will set you apart from most people.

Though I am less outgoing than Brian and networking is normally outside of my comfort zone, I strive to surround myself with people who are contributors to the world. We draw certain people to us, and that's our natural network. The members of your network will want to introduce you to their networks as well.

Who are you choosing to learn from? Your mentors should be results-oriented trailblazers. Who is helping you with your vision? Your team is a reflection of your organization. It's important they understand your purpose and vision and are aligned with it. Who you spend time with is a reflection of who you are. Be confident but not arrogant. Stay humble and people will want to work with you.

Remember that the like-minded people you choose to surround yourself with don't have to be in your backyard. They can be anywhere on the planet, thanks to the Internet.

If you're in environments that are negative or toxic, remove yourself from them or else see what you can do to influence an environment to make it a lot more positive and supportive and contribute to the greater good.

Be the Person You Really Want to Become

If you want a really good friend, be a really good friend. That philosophy translates into business: if you want a really good client, be a really good client.

In my professional and personal dealings, I try to help anybody I can without asking for anything in return. I've found that people help me without asking for anything in return. Life really is a mirror of who and what and how you are.

We talk about what makes life easy. The bottom line: don't get overwhelmed. Take one step at a time. Just keep at it while being the person you want to be. Be the person you want to surround yourself with; once you are, you will attract those kinds of people into your circle.

You could literally increase your network by 10 times by getting involved in different programs in which you can meet and connect with like-minded people. I often hear folks in my Best Seller Mega Minds program, which is a mastermind program, talk about the value they are receiving by connecting with the other people in the program.

However you choose to connect with people, remember that if you want a friend, be a friend. This is another mantra to keep repeating on a daily basis. Brian and I have friends all over the world. It really doesn't matter where you are. You can build your network from anywhere.

Know When to Enlist Your Relay Team

When you consider what any of us really wants to accomplish in life, it's all made easier when we have networks and friends and people of influence to rely on.

A relay team is composed of trusted people who you can pass the baton of responsibility to when necessary. These are either people you hire to perform certain tasks or people in your network with skills you need who are willing to volunteer their time and expertise. Continue to do the tasks that you're really good at but pass the baton to someone who has expertise in other parts of your business.

Do What You Love and the Money Will Follow

It comes down to realizing your passion. What is that passion and how do you know? It's a question we keep asking in this book.

If you find that you're doing tasks that aren't in alignment with your passion or what you truly love, you will quickly know because everything will feel tedious. It's going to feel like drudge work. Pay close attention to what it is that you're doing and pay equally close attention to whether you love your work. You can fool yourself for only so long before the reality of your relationship to your work finally sets in.

If you don't love what you're doing, can you change your attitude and learn to love it? It's certainly possible, but you may find that it's really challenging to do. You have to dramatically shift your consciousness to make that work.

I'm fortunate to be doing work that I deeply love. I don't feel like I ever work a day in my life because I'm in that place of passion for what I do.

You're not going to succeed at everything. No one does, of course. Every once in a while, what you're doing isn't going to work. When that happens, the key is to get back up and keep going. With the right attitude, you will win.

Whatever it is that you've chosen to do as an income generator, you should always want to take it to the next level. If you can't inspire yourself to do that, you've probably lost your passion for it.

Spend one hour on the phone with three or four other inspirational, powerful, positive types of people and brainstorm with them. You will come up with all kinds of useful ideas that are unavailable to you if you're working in isolation. Surround yourself with people you can share those ideas with and build on them.

Success loves company a lot more than misery does.

Your Darn Easy Assignment #1
Make Yourself Accountable

Recruit an accountability buddy and send that person your accomplishment list at the beginning of each week. Make sure the person you enlist is reliable and trustworthy.

Encourage your buddy to keep his or her own accomplishment list to share with you so that you truly are partnering in this exercise.

Go through your list every day and record your accomplishments.

Check in with your accountability partner during the middle of the week and again at the end of the week. Let your partner know how you are doing with your checklist. If that person is partnering with you, review his or her checklist.

Make this entire experience positive and supportive of each other. Do this exercise without judgment. Don't criticize or ridicule yourself or your partner. Be compassionate.

Brainstorm ways you and your accountability partner can help each other fulfill the goals on your respective lists. Think of yourselves as a team.

Keep this accountability exercise going. Do it for as long as you can. Ideally, it will last as long as your goals remain unachieved.

Your Darn Easy Assignment #2
Focus on Your Outcomes

Every morning, write out in longhand your accomplishment and accountability lists for that day. This is intended to keep you focused on your desired outcomes.

In addition to writing out that list every morning, add points and ideas for actions you will take that day to move this goal farther along toward accomplishment.

PART IV

Guarantee Sustainability, Growth, and Greater Ease

See yourself living in abundance and you will attract it.
It works every time, with every person.

—BOB PROCTOR

Renew Your Commitment to Growth

Develop a commitment to do whatever it takes to make your business grow. Work through a targeted list every day with focused energy to support and reinforce commitment. This comes back to awareness. It's also about our own personal growth, not just revenue growth. Commitment to growth becomes a habit. It becomes a code of conduct over time. Who do you know who can help you grow your business?

Identify Your Areas of "Genius-ness" and Weakness

Trying harder isn't necessarily the way to succeed more. All of us are born with certain talents that can become strengths when we add skills or knowledge. It's important that we recognize what we are naturally good at and work on enhancing those talents. In business, your life will be much easier when you tap into what you are good at. Find people who have strengths where your weaknesses are. Notice your results and how you feel when you approach certain tasks. Whatever feels more like play than work to you is where you'll find your strengths. There are certain traits that define successful entrepreneurs.

Find Pain Relievers

Treat the tough times as an adventure about which you will one day reminisce. If you are having a tough time and not feeling good about something, you need to find someone you can trust who will help you get through it. Share it not to bring that person down but to get a different perspective that will help you expand your own. Stop doing what you don't enjoy. If it's painful and you do it anyway, you are sabotaging yourself. You will harbor destructive or negative emotions as a result. Either adjust to the people and the situation or remove yourself from that situation.

Plan Balance for Your Life

If you're having fun at what you're doing, you're more likely to become a success. Set aside time for whatever makes you happy. You can get swallowed up by your business, and so you need to plan for balance. Your work time can become more productive in less time if you plan on doing something you really enjoy. That puts you in a much better head space. Put into your business plan opportunities to recharge yourself physically and mentally. Create relaxing settings to enhance productivity. Add healthy doses of fun. When you have balance, you are more enjoyable to be around.

Calculate Bottom Line Dollars and Sense

Be smart about your expenses, taxes, and bill payments. Many business owners are choking at the end of the year because of big tax payments when they could have budgeted for those payments every month. Invest money in the business only when that makes sense. Why pay for office space if you can work out of your home? Ensure that every expenditure works to extend the reach and growth of your business. Grow your business by paying bills promptly. Break your business expenses down to the smallest components.

Drive Your Financial Income with Emotional Income

If you focus on emotional income—what makes you feel good about what you're doing—it enables business growth because the focus is on giving rather than receiving. Clients and customers will be attracted to you. Having and expressing passion for your business helps attract abundance. Find ways to make a positive difference in the lives of your customers and clients.

Cultivate the Law of Compensation

You will be compensated in proportion to the good you are delivering. How can you contribute to improving someone else's life? How can you make people feel better about themselves? It requires just a simple switch in the way you think. The law of attraction is about attracting more, whereas the law of compensation is about what you can contribute. Always ask yourself, "How can I serve in greater ways?"

Practice Psychological Reciprocity

Give people something without any expectation of return; it's a natural response for them to want to give back in return. Reciprocity comes about because people feel inspired to give back. The law of compensation is about service you provide, whereas psychological reciprocity entails giving without any expectation of receiving in return. It's an energy you project to attract more of the same.

Daily Disciplines for a Life with Ease

Create results-oriented disciplines for daily use. Make a list of what you want to accomplish each day to be more productive. The things you do every single day are the disciplines that move you and your business forward. Write in a gratitude journal. Do positive affirmations. Daily physical exercise will give you more energy and make you feel better about yourself. When you are exercising, think about what you want to accomplish that day. The stronger your body is, the better you will feel about yourself. Don't take yourself too seriously. Send good vibes to those who bother you. These are success habits that will put you in a mindset for success.

Your Darn Easy Assignment #1: Create New Positive Habits for Success

Your Darn Easy Assignment #2: Don't Break the Chain

Renew Your Commitment to Growth

In Part I, we discussed a dynamic young Internet-based business owner, Anik Singal, who gave out copies of his e-book to raise his company's profile. His firm, VSS Mind Media, Inc., teaches entrepreneurs how to market on the Internet and generate more traffic and, with it, profits. It's a more than $12 million a year education company selling webinar courses, software, and tools to make life easier for entrepreneurs and small business owners.

What Anik practices at his company and teaches others how to create is guaranteed sustainability and growth while experiencing greater ease. It's a darn easy approach that enables you to multiply your profits as you cut the time you might normally spend on your business venture.

Anik shared with us some of his tips for success. It all starts with putting your entire business, to whatever extent possible, on the Internet: "It's easier to find that balance for your life when your business is based on the Internet. Almost everything you do to make money on the Internet can be automated. There is a lot of 'set it and forget it.' People still buy your stuff while you are asleep. This is far superior to a brick and mortar business. Automation makes your business life much easier.

"The only way to multiply your hours in the day is to remove yourself from the picture. The less important you make yourself to the business, sometimes the better it becomes. How can you remove yourself from the business and make your life easier? Ease is not having to be physically in one place. I work from my home in Maryland. I have employees in Eastern Europe, Singapore, all over the United States. One person has been with me for eight years, and I have never met him."

Anik says the biggest challenge of having employees work from home is that they must be super motivated. How do you ensure that? It starts with the hiring process. He concentrates on hiring people who already have experience working out of their homes or away from corporate office structure. They need to possess the capacity to be so focused that the distractions of home life don't bother them.

Once they are on his team, he keeps them and his company on track by using a central project management system. "We test each other. We keep everybody in the loop about the whole company. We do periodic team calls every few weeks or once a month. We give a lot of recognition, so employees get satisfaction, and that helps to build company culture and morale. We don't go cheap; we pay market rates. We look for track records in employees. Everyone on my team has passion and loves what we are doing. They love their jobs, and when the company does well, they get bonuses and more compensation. They must be team players.

"Never say, 'That's not my job' is a core value of my company. We have a fire room where people can call for help and our other employees respond and step in. We have a lot of camaraderie. When employees are in it for the bigger picture, they work harder. They care about the other team members. They care about their company. They care about profits and growth."

You need to step out and really start taking a look at your business from a different angle so that you can try new approaches to growth. Whether it's developing a focus on selling your services or products on the Internet or developing an entirely new model of structure and growth for your enterprise, this is the time to start.

Not everything you try is going to work, of course, but by trying new radical, completely out of the box ways to stimulate growth in your revenue, you can quantum jump your business from where it is now to where you want it to be.

To begin that process, you must first realize whether you're locked in to a losing strategy that can be the death of your endeavors.

Price Prichett has a doctorate in psychology and advises CEOs and other business leaders on strategies for organizational change. He tells the following story in his book *You 2: A High Velocity Formula for Multiplying Your Personal Effectiveness in Quantum Leaps* to illustrate the trap that many business owners fall into:

Price was sitting in a hotel room "listening to the desperate sounds of a life-or-death struggle going on a few feet away. There is a small fly burning out the last of its short life energies in a futile attempt to fly through the glass of the window pane.

"The whining wings tell the fly's strategy: try harder. But it's not working. The frenzied effort offers no hope for survival. Erratically, the struggle is part of the trap. It is impossible for the fly to try hard enough to succeed at breaking through the glass. Nevertheless, this little insect has staked its life on reaching its goals through raw effort and determination. This fly is doomed. It will die there on the windowsill.

"Across the room, ten steps away, the door is open. Ten seconds of flying time and this small creature could reach the outside world it seeks. With only a fraction of the effort now being wasted, it could be free of this self-imposed trap. The breakthrough possibility is there. It would be so easy. Why doesn't the fly try another approach, something dramatically different? How did it get so locked in on the idea that this particular route, and determined effort, offer the most promise for success? What logic is there in continuing, until death, to seek a breakthrough with 'more of the same'?"

This story gives us a strong message about how we can get ourselves in a rut and beat ourselves to death against whatever obstacle confronts us even when a simple path could be nearby, easily accessible to us if only we would widen the scope of our view. Sometimes all the difference in the world can be made by a commitment to do things a little differently than our habits have programmed us to do it.

For many book authors, trying to market one's own book can be a frustrating experience, much like that fly banging repeatedly up against a window. I had a client who decided to make her own book a bestseller. The day before her book launch, she went to a website and found the names of editors and agents and sent them 400 personalized e-mails basically saying, "I am Elle Newmark and I'm doing this book campaign. You're going to see my book on the Best Sellers List. I'm looking for a publisher. If you're interested, get back in touch with me."

Some people might hear about her approach and respond, "I would never do that," or, "I would never be capable of doing that." If you are one of those people, if you cling to that attitude, you will never enjoy the benefits such an approach can bring. You're sabotaging yourself if you can't or won't imagine yourself committed to going beyond your usual habits and comfort zone.

Elle Newmark landed a contract from Simon & Schuster for $2.4 million for her book. Why? She took a risk. She tried something new. She went a little bit further in her commitment to trying a new bold approach.

When I'm working with my clients on how to reach out and connect with partners and potential partners, I often tell them to send personalized correspondence. You will get a much better response by doing so. Elle went through my program about how to make your book a bestseller, and she took that advice several steps further in her commitment to grow her book sales.

Elle baked cookies shaped like a dog bone (I suspect she did so because her book was called *Bones of the Dead*), packaged them, and sent them by courier to potential promotional partners. She was looking to get people to help and support her in the marketing of her book.

She sent out those cookies with a note saying, "Hey, I'm Elle Newmark. I'm doing this campaign for my book. I'm really looking for your support."

It wasn't that what she did was dramatically different from what some other authors have done. It was the way she approached people that was truly unique. She happened to be a great baker and her cookies were delicious, and she got a tremendous response of support from taking this little extra step toward making new connections. It produced extraordinary results for her.

Our goal in this book is to inspire you to make a commitment to do whatever it takes to make your business grow. Keep in mind that it's not just about revenue growth. It's about your personal growth and your commitment to doing things differently when necessary.

It becomes a code of conduct over time. When Elle took those steps to grow her sales, she learned a lot about what she was capable of doing comfortably and with ease, and that has benefited her with more success ever since.

Ask yourself where you can renew your commitment to growth:

What risks have I *not* taken to grow my business?
What is really holding me back from taking those risks?
Who do I know who can help me reach beyond my comfort zone?

Identify Your Areas of "Genius-ness" and Weakness

All of us are born with certain talents. Those talents can become strengths when we add skills or knowledge. A lot of people try to be like other people and become upset if they aren't talented in certain areas.

Someone may have a natural gift for music, for instance, and someone else for accounting or bookkeeping. It's important that we recognize what we are naturally good at and work on enhancing those talents. That is our genius-ness.

Build on your strengths, not on your weaknesses. A lot of people try to build a skill around a weakness, and that's one of the worst things you can do. You will never be good at it, and the time and resources you spend on trying can undermine your business.

Find people who are really good at whatever you are weakest at. Once you build a team, you can create greater opportunities for success and do so with ease.

Notice your results and how you feel when you approach certain tasks. What do you have the most fun doing? What feels more like play than work? What are the tasks that you try to avoid and that fill you with dread?

Your answers to these questions will help establish your strengths. Everything else may fall in the category of your weaknesses.

Trying Harder Isn't Necessarily the Solution for Greater Success

Trying harder may not offer any real promise for getting what you want out of life. Sometimes, in fact, trying harder is a big part of the problem. If you tie your hopes for a breakthrough on simply trying harder than ever, you may harm or even kill your chances for success.

We wrote earlier about how important it is to surround yourself with good, trustworthy people. In fact, and we can't emphasize this enough, it is vitally important to surround yourself with good, talented, and reliable people.

Present to others what your business is about, what you're doing, and where you need help. Encourage them to give you suggestions about what they think you can do rather than just try harder, because we can get stuck sometimes in our own rut of who and what we think we should be. Others could give us a whole different outlook that could radically change our business.

Are you really doing what you love? If you are not, could you eventually fall in love with what you're doing? We keep coming back to this theme because a lot of people in the corporate world do things they don't particularly love. That's no secret, and we see the evidence of it in the high stress levels that physicians report finding in their business world patients.

There is a way of managing through the stress and creating more ease until you get to the point where you are really doing what you love. It's a transition approach.

Years ago, when I first became an author, I attended an event that Mark Victor Hansen put on called Mega Book Marketing. Arielle Ford, an author and literary agent, was one of the speakers. I didn't know Arielle at that time; since then we've become very close friends. Arielle said to the audience, "If you're an author, don't quit your day job." In other words, find a way to transition to your desired business while you're still making reliable money in other areas. If necessary, do your business part-time until it generates enough income for you to do it full-time.

I wrote the book *Be a Dog with a Bone* because I realized that as an author, if you want to be successful, you've got to be like a dog with a bone. Be tenacious and be ferocious, but it's also important to be really clear about what it is that you love doing and remind yourself of that every day.

By taking my own advice, I shifted my business primarily to teaching, speaking, and mentoring. These were the three areas that I loved the most and was great at. They were my true passions. I had been teaching since I was 20 years old.

My business grew even more. I believe that happened because I tapped into what I was really good at and what I really loved. When you do that, your business can soar as mine did.

When you're out doing something you really like, you're going to get good at it. Your business will grow because of the skill sets you are developing.

Brian also had a piece of his business that brought in pretty good income, but he didn't enjoy it. There was a real hassle associated with it. He wasn't getting that all-important emotional income. Therefore, he dropped it. Much as it happened with me, doing so gave him more time to zero in on the tasks he enjoyed and the things he was better at, and his business grew because of that decision.

There are certain tasks we definitely need to do that may be tedious and joyless, but a lot of that can be contracted out to others.

You don't have to hire full-time or even part-time employees. There are inexpensive virtual assistants available.

Once you contract out what you don't enjoy or what takes up too much of your time, you become more free to focus on what you are good at and what you most enjoy. That newly freed up ease will also help you build your business.

Traits That Define Successful Entrepreneurs

If you read articles about successful entrepreneurs, such as those that appear in *Forbes* and other business publications, you come away with seven or so frequently mentioned traits that every entrepreneur should have or be able to develop as part of his or her genius-ness.

Here they are in no particular order:

1. **Risk taking.** You can't be risk-averse if you want entrepreneurial success. You can't value financial security above success, you must accept that there are no guarantees, and you must be comfortable taking action without a safety net. When you are on that netless tightrope, don't look down or behind. Stay focused on the goal straight ahead of you.
2. **Tenacity.** Your road to success is a marathon, and you need stamina to get to the finish line. You know the old saying "Persistence pays." To summon tenacity, you need fortitude and seemingly boundless energy (which is often fueled by your passion for what you're doing).
3. **Passion.** Your commitment to your vision and your faith in your eventual success have to be resolute. You must care deeply. You must be hard-core about it. From this reservoir of caring and commitment you will draw sustenance, energy from your passion, to propel you toward your goal.

4. **Adaptation.** You must be able to adapt quickly to unforeseen situations and problems. You can't allow yourself to become mired in procrastination or fear. This ability, which is particularly useful in new ventures, is called pivoting, and it's an essential quality when new approaches are necessary to avoid failure.

5. **Trustworthiness.** You must be reliable. People need to know they can depend on you. You must also trust yourself to be true to your word. All relationships are built on trust, especially in doing business with others. You may have heard the expression "Investors don't invest in companies; investors invest in people." This means that investors want their money only in good, trustworthy hands.

6. **Confidence.** You must trust your idea no matter how crazy it may sound to others. It's normal to have doubts, but you can't allow those doubts to metastasize and undermine your trust in yourself and your business idea.

7. **Intuition.** Logic and planning will take you only so far. Success often depends on heightened awareness and being able to size up people and situations quickly and accurately when good information is in short supply. Sharp intuition enables you to take advantage of opportunities—the gut hunch—when you don't have time to engage in extensive analysis.

Find Pain Relievers

Many people go into business believing that it's going to be a sacrifice that involves giving up their health or their family or their relationships to create success. It doesn't have to be that way. You only need to shift your attitude about what success requires. Being in business for yourself can offer you so much success and freedom, both time and money freedom, that it will amaze you.

Thinking that creating more success in your life will be a painful process is just an idea. It's a toxic thought— and it's contagious. It's something that you made up, and it doesn't have to be that way.

If you're having a tough time or not feeling good about something regarding your income or business, find someone you can trust who will help you get through it. Share your experience to get a different perspective. In the process, you will be expanding your own perspective, and that will help you meet the challenge.

Treat the Tough Times as an Adventure

Whenever Brian gets into situations that are really tough or feel like a struggle, he doesn't dwell on the negative aspects. He looks at the situation as an adventure. He asks himself a simple question: "What can I learn from this situation?"

If you look back on your life, all the things you've had to go through—and we've all been through tough times—you probably remember how some of it was tough but that it wasn't as bad as you thought it was at the time. Nothing ever is. If you change the way you look at the hardships, treat life as an adventure, and go into it with a smile, you and your business will come out way better.

I've had experiences in my own business in which I've launched initiatives and they haven't gone as well as I thought or expected. At other times I've had an idea for a product and gotten it all ready only to realize that I didn't really want to do it. Sometimes this was followed by the discovery of an even better idea or a product with greater value.

When you learn to look at every situation differently and do that habitually, it becomes second nature over time. Even if it's something that wasn't pleasant or enjoyable and you have negative emotions come up, look back on it and ask, "What's great about this experience? What can I learn from this? How can I do it differently next time?"

Questions cause us to shift our focus. If we ask ourselves better questions, we're going to get better answers. What it also does is condition us to have an even better experience the next time we go through something similar.

Another pain reliever is to find specific ways to inject more enjoyment into your business. One of the things I started doing many years ago was to put humor in my newsletter. I've been doing my newsletter for about 13 years. I send one out a couple of times a month, sometimes every week. Do you know how rare it is to find jokes that are clean and not offensive? It's fun looking for jokes. It puts a smile on my face. It also really lightens the joke recipient's day. People write me and say, "I look forward to receiving your newsletter because I love your jokes." It's a way I can inject more enjoyment into other people's lives.

The biggest pain reliever, of course, is to stop doing what you don't enjoy. If it's painful and you do it anyway, you are sabotaging yourself by sapping your energy. You will harbor destructive or negative emotions as a result.

Either adjust to the people or situation or remove yourself from the situation temporarily or permanently. Find a way to transition into a job area you enjoy more. If you don't like where you're going, change the direction.

Plan Balance for Your Life

Brian lives by the philosophy that if you're having fun, you're going to be a success. To enjoy what you're doing and have a good time with your work, you've got to make sure you're working with people you want to work with, people who you know you can have fun with and who appreciate good humor without going overboard.

When you're in that lighthearted frame of mind, you attract more to you. Your business will grow because people want to deal with you and be around you.

There's a restaurant that Brian frequents. It doesn't have the best food, but the owner is one of the nicest guys Brian has ever met. He always makes Brian feel at home, and Brian frequents the place because of the vibe.

You don't need to have the best or most efficient or most economical business in your field, but if you have fun and enjoy the people you're dealing with, you're going to keep attracting business because people will enjoy how they feel around you and your employees. A stressed-out workaholic isn't someone most people want to be around.

Being lighthearted helps you achieve balance in your life. Balance is something that Brian and I believe is personal. It must be tailored to your particular nature and circumstances. It's not a cookie-cutter way of being that you fit yourself into snugly.

Ask yourself what it is that you are loving—or trying to love—and whether it is making you feel enthusiastic and playful or somber and anxiety-ridden. If you're energized, feeling good, and paying attention to how you're feeling, you're also making progress and checking the milestones (those check marks on your list that indicate the progress you are making). The joy you give and receive from your work is one of those milestones, as is seeing the fulfillment of tasks and accomplishments along the way to a goal.

Sometimes you have to plan on creating balance in your life because you can get swallowed up in business and all of its mundane details. Keep reminding yourself that your work time can become more productive in less time if you plan on doing something you really enjoy. That puts you in a much better head space to tackle the challenges when they arise.

For me, it's only been in the last year that I've made a conscious decision to have fun with my work. I put it in my goal statements. It's in the script I listen to when I'm talking about how incredible my life is. It's something I focus on when I'm creating my accountability report of what I'm going to accomplish every single week, which may include, for instance, "I will generate X dollars of new revenue this week." I've found that a focus on healthy doses of fun has really added much more joy to my life.

Do you assume that having balance in your life means spending eight hours a day sleeping, eight hours a day socializing, and eight hours a day working? Is that slice-up of your day or some similar division your idea of having a balanced life?

Put into your business plan opportunities to recharge yourself physically and mentally. Create relaxing settings to enhance productivity. Establish quality time for yourself. Pace yourself. Both Brian and I have a relaxed lifestyle, yet we are highly productive because we've learned and practice balance. When you have balance and plan balance into your schedule, you're a more enjoyable person to be around.

A long time ago, I made a conscious decision that my weekends are going to be family time. They're not always family time because deadlines and circumstances can unexpectedly intervene. But normally, weekends are my opportunity to recharge and reconnect with my spouse and family.

It really comes down to paying attention to how you're using your time. It's not necessarily a time management issue but a matter of how you are managing yourself and how you are feeling. Sometimes you do not need to recharge your batteries with renewed energy and enthusiasm for your goals because you already have that in abundance. Monitor yourself. And make sure you recharge as necessary.

Bob Proctor is doing what he loves. I watch this man, who is in his eighties, on stage and I'm not only amazed at what he's saying, I'm amazed at the level of energy he puts into it. I am constantly awed by the love he has for his work and the way he displays it. You know he has incredible passion for what he's doing. For him, balance isn't dividing the day by three or any other multiple. It's a balance that just feels good to him. It's something that works well for him.

Brian loves fishing and motorcycling. He may have a long day at work, but he always makes sure to take time to do what grounds him. That could be fishing or going out on his motorcycle and letting go of all the accumulated stress and worries. Doing whatever it is that makes you happy can pay unquantifiable dividends for your business. Make it a priority.

Always set aside some time to do what makes you happy and what puts your core at peace because if you do that consistently, you will be a happier being. You will be somebody people want to work with and want to do business with because you have—and you will project to others— that healthy balance in your work and your life.

A Bad Attitude Can Ruin It for Everyone

Once I was on a flight from Toronto, and the flight attendant taking care of the guests in first class was obviously not very happy. It looked like he didn't enjoy his job. First class is supposed to be all about good service, and this airline employee seemed to have forgotten that part of his training.

There was a point at which I really wanted a glass of water, and the person beside me ended up buzzing the flight attendant to get us a drink of water. The attendant had never asked us what we wanted. It felt like our presence was disturbing him. It wasn't a pleasant flight.

Flying home from Dallas was completely different. The service was outstanding, complemented by lots of smiles from the flight attendants. The attendants kept asking if there was anything we wanted or needed. What a difference! The difference lay in how much fun the flight attendant was having and how contagious that became for the passengers. It certainly created a positive experience for me, and of course, it helped redeem the airline in my eyes because the better service I received on the return flight helped soften my memory of the prior negative experience.

You want to foster positive lasting memories of you and your services in your clients. Word-of-mouth marketing is the most effective marketing, and maintaining a high level of courteous, friendly, efficient service helps ensure that you remain well regarded and well spoken of.

You may find, as I have, that there are times when others will want you to recommend them to your clients and for some reason—not necessarily something you can put your finger on—it doesn't feel right to do so. Somehow you sense that the person who wants a recommendation doesn't have the right attitude or won't be a good fit with your client. Trust those gut instincts.

Quite often you will find that your intuition was on target long before your logic or your experience yielded something negative to focus on. If you recommend someone who turns out to be a bad call or a detriment to your client's business relations, that decision could come back to haunt you.

Calculate Bottom Line
Dollars and Sense

A young woman who was making over $1 million a year with her business sought my advice. I asked her a series of questions: What's your profit level? Are you paying yourself? Are you getting a living wage? Those questions were a challenge for her. Even though on the surface she had what seemed to be a successful business, the profit wasn't there. She wasn't able to pay herself. She was basically working for free.

There have been times when I started new businesses and wasn't paying myself. That was fine . . . for a while. I had an assistant, and she made more the first year than I did. It was part of the sacrifice in my commitment to build the business. But there will come a time, sooner than you think, when if you're going to stay in business, you will need to pay yourself. You can't sacrifice your livelihood to a position of permanent, unsustainable debt.

You need to be smart and careful about your expenses, taxes, and bill payments. Many business owners are choking at the end of the year because of the big tax payments they must make, when they could have budgeted for those payments and put the money aside every month. Making those monthly or quarterly tax payments requires discipline, but so does achieving success.

Fiscal responsibility is mostly common sense. For example, as a daily practice, make sure your expenditures extend the reach of your business so that you can grow it further.

Challenge every expense with a series of questions. Why maintain office space, for example, if you can work out of your home? Are you getting good leads or referrals? Are you getting the results you're looking for? If you're not, there could be a kink in the hose. There could be something that's blocking you.

Even if you're a solopreneur—an entrepreneur working all by yourself—your expenses may not be that great at first, but if you want to grow your business, you'll need to start advertising, promoting, traveling, attending events, and building a website. All of that will result in mounting expenses, and so you need to have a handle on your cash flow long before you reach that point of expansion.

Map it out. I keep a spreadsheet. Yes, I have a bookkeeper. Yes, I have an accountant, and so it's never a surprise to me how much money I'm making in my business or where my profit level is. The bottom line is something I always keep my eye on.

Have a spreadsheet, and put in it your forecasts and your actual revenue and expenses. Track it all in detail. It's very easy to do once you get the hang of it.

These are all basics of Business 101 whether your business is large or small. As a business owner, it's really important for you to have a handle on every aspect of it. It's one of the foundations for success.

Grow Your Business by Paying Bills Promptly

Though no one should be surprised at what failing to pay bills on time will bring in terms of damage to your reputation and lost business, you may be surprised at the unexpected dividends that paying bills on time will bring.

Brian and I are fanatics about paying bills on time. Brian puts it this way: "When I get a bill in, I don't wait days to pay. I pay it immediately. I think it does two things. It clears your head, and it makes you feel good about yourself and the reputation you have. That will help your business grow, as crazy as that sounds, although it has nothing to do directly with business building."

Break It Down to the Smallest Components

Bob Proctor always has a calculator in his pocket. He is forever thinking up new projects, and when it comes to the financial side of it, he breaks it down to the tiniest components. Then he steps out and takes action.

This process is going to be different for everybody. Say you've got a monthly goal for business income. You start by dividing that number by the number of days in the month. Then you break it down to the number of hours in each day. You break it down to the point where it's almost ridiculous.

Once you see the overall goal in this tiny perspective, it's not so daunting and you can say more easily, "I can definitely do that." All you've got to focus on is doing that one piece each day or whatever period of time you've broken it down to. At first it seems almost ridiculous, but over time, having this perspective constantly in mind makes the entire goal more manageable.

Set your goals according to the kind of income you need to bring in. Ask yourself, "What must I do today that's going to bring in this amount of income?"

Focus on the now: "What can I do now, this very hour, this very minute, to generate the income I need to meet my goal?" If you keep the focus on the now, you'll see how the rest will take care of itself.

Drive Your Financial Income with Emotional Income

As we discussed earlier in the book, when Brian started Insight of the Day, he knew early on that it was going to be a great business. He realized that he had something special when he saw people starting to purchase some of the products online as a result of getting something free from him.

The feedback he received was the emotional income, and it enabled him to create an entire business model that turned into a moneymaking machine—but that wasn't the original intention.

Whatever it is that you're doing, make sure that you're making a difference in the lives of the people with whom you're doing business. It's as simple as that.

Brian makes careful choices about the kind of quotes he sends to people every day and the stories he uses on Fridays. For the quotes especially, he picks whatever resonates with him. He knows from experience that if it resonates with him, it's going to resonate with other people. He tries to find themes he knows can help people in the way they are looking at their day.

It doesn't matter what business you're in. If you can make a difference in the lives of the customers or clients you're dealing with, if you can somehow find even the smallest and simplest way to change the way they're looking at their day or their situation, this will translate into emotional income.

If you can find a way to do that within your business, your business is going to grow like crazy because it will become a heart-centered business. If you can take whatever it is that you're doing and build it in a heart-centered way by intentionally going out and helping people and changing lives, even if it's in the smallest way, your business is going to grow like you would never imagine.

If you focus on emotional income—what makes you feel good about what you're doing—it will enable your business to grow because the focus will be on giving rather than receiving. Business customers will be attracted to you because your passion for your business will help create abundance and that abundance will become clear and obvious to everyone.

Cultivate the Law of Compensation

You will be compensated in proportion to the good you are delivering. Ask yourself: "How can I contribute to improving someone else's life? How will I make people feel better about themselves?"

It's just a simple shift in the way you think, and it involves an understanding of the law of compensation.

The law of attraction is about attracting more of what you desire, whereas the law of compensation is about what you can contribute, what you can give back to others. Brian and I consider these to be natural laws. They've made a positive difference in our lives. Using them can make a difference in yours, too.

Under the law of compensation, the amount of money you earn will always be in an exact ratio to the demand for what you do, your ability to do it, and the difficulty in replacing you.

One of the things Bob Proctor came up with that really shifted his business and his life was the law of compensation and its focus on a person's ability to perform. Bob woke me up to this reality.

Whether you are an entrepreneur working for yourself, a small business owner, or an employee in a corporate environment, always ask yourself, "How I can serve in greater ways? How can I be more, give more, do more that's going to contribute to others?" The law of compensation has become a foundational premise for everything I do.

Practice Psychological Reciprocity

Maybe you've heard the story about the two dogs that walk into a room. One walks out happy and wagging its tail. The other walks out growling and nasty.

Somebody asks, "What is in that room that would make one dog happy and the other one unhappy?"

The answer: "It's a room full of mirrors."

Life is like that. We live in rooms of mirrors.

Whatever we are inside, that's what we see out there. We will attract the good if we're always putting good vibes out there. If we're putting out negativity, we're going to attract negativity. That's not to say that you don't attract negativity every once in a while—that's only natural—but to really be focused on the good and putting out good energy counteracts those instances in which negativity tries to ensnare you.

Whatever kind of energy you're putting out into the universe is going to come back to you, so make a conscious choice to always put out good. Always speak well of the people you work with. Don't focus on the negative.

Give others something without any expectation of return, and it's a natural response for them to want to give back to you. The law of compensation is about the service you provide, whereas psychological reciprocity is a matter of giving without any expectation of receiving in return.

In social psychology, psychological reciprocity refers to responding to a positive action by producing another positive action. Kind actions are rewarded with more kind actions. It's important to focus on this and keep the concept in mind as you interact with your employees, your clients, and your prospective clients.

For entrepreneurs or anyone in business, it's not only the business that we're working on, it's our own self-development and the way we're communicating with others. In this regard, I had an experience with a woman who was considered to be an expert in her field. I asked her a question about something. Her response was to laugh at me. I'm saying she really laughed at me. It wasn't one of those "Oh, that's kind of a funny question" laughs. It was one of those "What a stupid question you're asking me" kind of laughs.

That encounter prompted me to ask myself if I had ever done that to others and, if so, how they felt as a result. It reminded me of how important it is to treat people the way we want to be treated.

Brian has someone he has to do business with, and although this individual comes across as superfriendly, Brian always feels that he has a hidden agenda.

To detect those hidden agendas, we really have to be in touch with our feelings, which is to say our intuition. We also have to recognize that we exude and project whatever is going on within ourselves.

If we're going to project joy and happiness, we need to feel it in our core. Otherwise, this disconnection between how we think and feel and how we act is noticed by others, and that triggers doubts about our motives and overall trustworthiness. Though we agree with the popular adage "Fake it until you make it" and although some people are quite good at that, we feel that you can still sense intuitively if someone has a hidden agenda.

Each of us has something negative going on at some point. It's part of being human. There is no need to focus on it. Always consciously bring yourself back to focus on the positive. Remember, the more of the positive you keep looking at and thinking about, the more of the positive will come to you. It's such an important yet simple lesson.

Daily Disciplines for a Life with Ease

Those things you do every single day are the disciplines that can move you and your business ventures forward.

In my case, I grab my gratitude journal first thing in the morning and do affirmations. I wouldn't think of going anywhere without doing that. I have a power life script, a document I wrote in which I scripted my life as if I were living my dream life. It's an emotionally charged description about 25 minutes long that I recorded and listen to.

Going to the gym early in the morning every day is one of Brian's disciplines. He does that after doing his gratitude journal. By 6:30 a.m., he is on his way to the gym. It gives him more energy and makes him feel better about himself. That hour in the gym each morning is also an opportunity for him to think about what he wants to accomplish that day. It's a routine that gets both his mind and his body in order.

The stronger your body is, the better you will feel about yourself. If you can't keep your body and your health strong, you'll have a problem achieving and maintaining any level of success in business or in life.

Each night Brian sits down and writes six things that he's going to initiate and accomplish the next day. He'll sit down the next morning and start to mark those things off his list. That's a discipline that he's created in his life, and it keeps him moving forward.

Create some disciplines for yourself that you're sure you're willing to follow through on. Make sure that you have your goals written down and that you've got them in front of you whenever possible. Create an outcome-based list. You're measuring things and noticing what's working. You're following through and focusing on your goals in everything that you're doing.

These are success habits. They put you into a mindset for success.

We have shared multiple results-oriented disciplines in this book that you can adopt to create greater ease and more success in your life. It's important that you put them into practice. We want you to think about what you're learning and make sure to follow through. Otherwise, it's an opportunity lost.

Don't Take Yourself So Seriously

We talk a lot about having fun because so many people take themselves so seriously that it undermines their effectiveness. That constant seriousness drives away business. It deadens the human spirit.

Sometimes it's the silly things that you do that can put a big smile on your face and enjoyment in your day. Being able to summon at will those lighthearted moments also makes everything go faster and relieves the tedium.

As Brian is walking around, he is consciously smiling or will do a kooky little dance. It sounds funny and maybe a little weird, but sometimes it's these spontaneous frivolous activities that can change your whole outlook on the day (and also the outlook of the people who witness your antics).

Make a conscious effort to have fun with what you're doing. Your body will release endorphins, the feel-good hormones.

When you make yourself and others smile and laugh, you're definitely going to experience greater ease in whatever you're doing.

Your Attitude Is a Choice You Make and Can Make One of the Single Biggest Differences in Your Success

It can be a subtle shift, or you can move it at the snap of your fingers. You can change your attitude about something that slowly or that quickly.

Switching to a much more positive attitude or outlook on your business and your life is a skill you can learn. There are many ways to go about it. If willpower alone isn't sufficient for you to shift spontaneously, you can learn any number of mindfulness techniques in instructional videos available on the Internet. Search under the term "mindfulness" or "mindfulness meditation" to learn what this ancient and effective technique is all about.

Feeling more relaxed and more at ease is a choice we make. We really have, or we can develop, the freedom to choose the way we react to things and the way we look at things. The more aware we are of that, the more quickly we can get out of a bad attitude that's harming our relationships and our business. It certainly makes living a lot easier.

Gratitude Isn't an End unto Itself; It's Where Everything Begins

Two decades ago, I started a daily practice of writing in a gratitude journal. As I indicated earlier in the book, there isn't a single morning when I don't get up and write in my gratitude journal. It's a practice and it's a habit. I grab the journal before I do anything. I have a rule: I don't look at my e-mails. I don't do anything else until I write in my gratitude journal. By focusing on what I am grateful for, I start the day off on a beautiful note.

There are some entries in my gratitude journal that haven't happened yet. There are some items that are constant, such as my wonderful relationships with my terrific husband, Denis, my son, and my grandson, including their health, safety, and prosperity. I may experience these all the time, but I don't take any of it for granted and still give thanks for them.

Expressing gratitude not only can set the tone for your day but also can help you deal with challenging situations. If something's not happening the way you want, if you're looking to create something and the obstacles feel overwhelming, put yourself in the attitude of gratitude and you will often find the solutions you need.

Express gratitude for the achievement of your goals even if it's not yet reality, even if there is no evidence for it yet. Having that frame of mind will completely change the way you look at your day, your life, your business, and everything going on around you. Some days it may be tougher to find something to be grateful for. Other days it's really easy. With practice, it always becomes easier to recognize the blessings that surround you.

If you get up every morning and start by making a list of what you're grateful for, it completely alters the way you move forward in your day. It will make your business better. It will make your relationships better. It will make absolutely everything better. It may seem like a silly exercise, but it is one of the key ingredients in being able to experience a great, successful, happy life.

One of my author clients created a separate gratitude journal and wrote in it three times a day something along the lines of "I'm so happy and grateful now that a big publishing house has picked up my book." She wrote out that gratitude statement 20 times in the morning, 20 times at noon, and 20 times at night.

That's a big commitment. I've done that. It's not a regular practice for me, but it's something I've done. It really puts you in a feeling state that yields its own rich bounty of rewards.

Let people know what you're grateful for and what you like about them. Always share this with the people you work with or deal with. Let them know what you think of them because that will alter their day in a positive way, but just as important, it will alter your own day.

Take all the advice in this book and integrate it into your life, apply its principles, and then share your experiences with us. We would love to hear about your success and how you're creating greater ease in your life. Contact us at peggy@peggymccoll.com and brian@proctorgallagher.com.

From our hearts to yours, we wish you even more success because we know you deserve it.

Your Darn Easy Assignment #1
Create New Positive Habits for Success

Weight Watchers is a program that has been successful because people have to periodically check in with others regarding their progress. This constant monitoring becomes a habit that reinforces the development of other positive habits, all with the goal of achieving and maintaining weight loss.

What sorts of new habits can you create to help you achieve your goals? These need to be habits that you can fit into your life and perform daily.

Write out a list of what you want to accomplish each day and make that a habit, a daily discipline. This will make you more productive.

Write up a daily discipline sheet. Use it as a tool. List three or four new habits you can create to start every day in a more productive fashion.

Think about how you can make these habits a normal part of your routine. How can you keep your commitment to sticking with these positive habits? Experiment with these habits. See which ones work best for you.

Your Darn Easy Assignment #2
Don't Break the Chain

Not only was the comedian Jerry Seinfeld an extraordinary performer and writer of comedic material, the daily technique he used to assure his own productivity demonstrated that he had the necessary vision and self-discipline to become a great success at a young age.

What Seinfeld practiced was a calendar system of goal achievement. His goal was to write at least one good joke a day, every day. On a wall, he mounted a large calendar showing every day of the year. When he accomplished his task of writing for that day, he placed a big X over the day with a red marker.

Over time, one big red X after another formed a chain on the wall. It was a constant visual reminder to keep the chain going and the goal achievements coming.

You can use the Seinfeld calendar in pursuit of any goal, whether it is meeting exercise goals or building a business. It's a daily call to maintain positive habits.

Get yourself a huge wall calendar for the year and apply your goals to it. Day by day, week by week, that chain of red Xs will tell you how far you've come and inspire you to keep the chain unbroken.

Appendix
Sample Visualization Transcript

E dit the following transcript, which is a version of my personal visualization exercise, and shorten it or lengthen it as you wish to fit your goals and circumstances. Write your name in the blanks and add your name and that of your business elsewhere in the transcript if you like.

When you record your transcript, remember to speak with emotive force as if you completely believe every word you are saying and there is passion behind the vision you hold for yourself.

Play this script back to yourself frequently. Listen to it while you are driving, listen through earphones while you are exercising, or play it back when you are relaxing at home. Think of it as your own private and portable booster club for the achievement of your goals.

I, _____(your name here)_____, am grateful to easily manifest all of my desires, and I am having fun doing so. I am a powerful creator of my dreams. I have authentically stepped into my power, and I am feeling great! Manifesting is *easy* for me, and I am totally grateful that I am manifesting easily, gracefully, honestly, ethically, legally, joyfully, and abundantly!

I naturally feel my goals into being. My goals are firmly planted in my subconscious mind. I see it, know it, and as a result manifest it easily.

I am in the spirit of opulence, and I think opulence, feel opulence, and experience opulence. I am grateful for opulence.

I recognize the eternal source of all riches, which always flourishes, and that source is within me. I am divinely guided in all my ways. Infinite intelligence is constantly revealing to me better ways to serve my fellow people, and I do serve my fellow people in better ways and am richly rewarded as a result.

I am guided, I am directed, and I *do* create and deliver exceptional and high-value products and services that bless and help humanity. I attract men and women who are spiritual, loyal, faithful, kind, honest, trustworthy, and talented and who contribute to the peace, prosperity, and progress of the world.

I am an irresistible magnet for good and attract fabulous wealth by giving the best quality of products and services.

I am constantly in tune with the infinite and the substance of wealth. Infinite intelligence governs all my plans and purposes, and I predicate all my success on the truth that God leads, guides, and governs me in all my undertakings.

I am at peace inwardly and outwardly at all times.

I am a tremendous success.

I am one with God, and God is always successful.

I am succeeding now.

I radiate love and goodwill to all those around me and to all my customers. I fill my mind and heart with God's love, power, and energy.

All those connected with me are spiritual and harmonious and connected in my growth, good, and prosperity. I give all honor and glory to God.

I am a very lucky person and feel grateful to be so lucky.

My inner thermostat is right on track as I am allowing an abundance of all good into my life—an abundance of love, an abundance of fun, an abundance of playfulness, an abundance of quality family time, an abundance of luxury, an abundance of money, an abundance of millions of dollars, an abundance of beauty, an abundance of health, an abundance of great energy, an abundance of profit, an abundance of money in my bank accounts, an abundance of net worth, an abundance of joy, an abundance of peace, an abundance of relaxation, and an abundance of gratitude—and it is all flowing beautifully into my life.

I am gratefully living my God-inspired life, totally fulfilled and very happy.

I choose to tune in to gratitude, and I express gratitude often.

My life just gets better and better every single day in every way.

I am ever grateful for God's riches that are active, ever present, eternal, and flowing in my life abundantly.

God's wealth is circulating in my life, and there always is a divine surplus. God's wealth flows to me in a rush of abundance, and I give thanks for my good now and for all of God's riches.

Wealth is mine now. God is the eternal source of my supply, meeting all of my needs at every instant.

I have absolute trust in God and all things good. I know that I am meeting all situations at all times, every time, and any time. God is my immediate source of supply, presenting me with all necessary ideas in the right way and at the right time. God's riches are ever flowing freely in my life, and there is *always* a divine surplus. As I repeat these truths and hear these truths, I know my mind is conditioned to receive divine supply forever flowing. Thank you.

God's love fills my soul, and I radiate love and goodwill to all. Wonderful miracles are happening in my life.

I love myself, and I take loving care of my body. I lovingly feed it nourishing food and beverages.

I lovingly groom it and dress it, and my body lovingly responds to me with vibrant health and energy. I love myself, and I provide for myself a beautiful and comfortable home that fills all my needs and my family's needs and is a pleasure to be in. I fill all the rooms with the vibration of love so that all who enter, myself included, feel this love and are nourished by it.

I love myself, and my work is truly enjoyable, using my talents and abilities, working with people whom I love and who love me, and earning a very healthy seven-figure income.

I love myself, and I behave in a loving way to all people, for I know that which I give returns to me multiplied. I attract only loving and appreciative people in my world.

I am a beloved child of the universe, and the universe lovingly takes care of me now and forevermore.

I, _____(your name here)_____, live a wonderful, harmonious, fun, relaxed, fully enjoyable, abundant, prosperous, rich, healthy, loving, and fulfilling life that I am very grateful for, and I say, "Thank you, God!"

Every day in every way I am getting better and better.

Every day in every way I am getting richer and richer.

My business continues to grow exponentially in revenue and profit. It is thriving and highly successful, *and* I am having fun.

I have the most amazing, talented, thoughtful, honest, brilliant accountant who is very accurate and good at what he does. He also saves me money and does an outstanding and perfect job with verifying my bookkeeping and my accounting. I am grateful for him. My bookkeeping and accounting are totally up to date, accurate, and honest.

I also have the most amazing personal assistant, who is exceptional. She is creative, energetic, smart, caring, and honest. She helps me immensely in my business. Since she joined my business, revenue has grown substantially, and I am so grateful to have her.

She has really helped me get more of the things done that I love to do and am really good at.

Personally, I have grown, become more, experienced more abundance, happiness, joy, health, laughter, and success, and I am so very grateful to be surrounded by opulence, luxury, and tranquillity.

I feel blessed to own my successful business. My business is hugely, widely, abundantly successful in serving the greater good.

My life is easygoing and fully enjoyable. I have a happy, healthy, rich, and abundant life.

I always have plenty of money to do whatever I want to do.

I am a very successful businessperson.

All my business and personal taxes are paid up, paid on time, and completely accurate.

I have such wonderful peace of mind. I love being so rich. I love being a multimillionaire. It feels great, and I love helping others, too.

I am a giver and give generously and freely.

I enjoy a high level of self-confidence. I feel really good about myself. I have a great sense of peace, and I am very calm. My success grows and gets better and better every day. I've taken a giant leap to success in every area of my life. I sleep better, feel better, look better, and enjoy even more abundance.

I am so grateful and happy my life is easy, relaxed, fun, happy, and healthy.

I gratefully own my vehicle outright.

I am enjoying and am grateful for my wonderful abundant and rich life, and I am grateful for my wonderful family and my perfect health!

I am a *very* happy and positive person, and I choose to be happy, and I choose to be positive all the time!

Since I feel so great, it attracts more wonderfulness into my life in so many wonderful ways!

I have the most amazing life, and I am so grateful for it. I am blessed in many ways.

I am grateful to do what I love and to love what I do.

I am gratefully, honestly, harmoniously, joyfully, easily enjoying an abundant and rich life.

I love that my life in every way goes well all the time.

I am successful in everything I do.

I gratefully and easily pay for all of my expenses.

I gratefully enjoy quality time with my family.

I easily bring out my inner and extraordinary gifts to the world—and feel blessed to do so. Others feel blessed, too!

I bring out the best in others, which makes them feel very happy and grateful.

I am making a positive and beneficial contribution to the lives of millions.

My success is absolutely guaranteed. My abundant wealth is guaranteed.

My life is amazingly wonderful, peaceful, smooth, easy, filled with love, full of love, and blessed—and all this is also guaranteed!

I have faith—absolute, complete faith—in myself! I believe in myself. I also have faith in the unknown, and I believe in my dreams and enjoy having them materialize in my life.

It feels so good to have so much money and to have more and more money flow continually into my life of abundance.

I always have plenty of money to do whatever I want to do.

We always have plenty of money to do whatever we want to do.

I am happily donating thousands of dollars to the organizations, individuals, and charitable programs that I love the most. I love having all this money to help others as well. It warms my heart to help others.

I am deserving of wealth. Being rich is a great thing. I *love* being rich. I am a happy and healthy multimillionaire. I have such a great comfort knowing I deserve it, too. And I appreciate it so much. Every day I appreciate and give thanks for the abundance in my life. I appreciate all the gifts that my wealth brings to my life.

I deserve the abundance that I enjoy. It is great for me to enjoy this abundance. I enjoy watching others enjoy it, too.

My abundant wealth is wonderful. I am financially set for life. What a great feeling this is.

I enjoy a great deal of quality time with my family and my friends. I enjoy time for relaxation, too.

I see myself, and I feel the elation of achieving great success!

I am happy with who I am. I love myself. I appreciate myself, and I treat myself in a loving way. I am love. I express love. I receive love. I am inspired! I am deserving, and I am worthy.

I am achieving and have achieved all of my goals and more, and it is all for the greater good. Thank you!

I am the happiest I've ever been in my life!

I have wonderful balance in my life.

Money comes easily to me, and for that and so many more things, I am so grateful.

God is the source of my supply, and *all* my needs are met at every moment of time and space. There is *always* a divine surplus, and God's wealth is forever circulating in my life.

I feel wonderful knowing that I am in amazing financial shape, and I feel the total peace and relaxation of being so rich. Thank you!

Every day for me starts with a warm happy feeling of gratitude. I wake up knowing and feeling very healthy. I feel that I am in outstanding physical condition. I feel loved. I feel loving. I am surrounded by loving, caring, giving, and wonderful people, and that feels so good, too. I am thrilled to be so rich. I am living a healthy, loving, wealthy, peaceful, opulent, joyful, and harmonious life.

I am walking in the inner silent knowing of the soul because I *know* in my heart that all my prayers and my desires are already answered, and I feel the reality of this in my heart.

I am attracting *only* peaceful people and peaceful events into my life.

I am attracting *only* loving people and loving events into my life.

I am attracting *only* harmonious people and harmonious events into my life.

I am attracting *only* wonderful clients into my life who are a joy to work with and who totally appreciate me and deeply love the help I offer them.

I know that everything is working out perfectly, beautifully, harmoniously, magnificently, smoothly, beneficially, magically, prosperously, with ease, as I desire, and for the good of all concerned.

I am definite about prosperity, and prosperity is definite about me. I enjoy prosperity every day in every way.

I am demonstrating the greatness within me, and others benefit from it, as do I. I am an instrument of God's peace and harmony. I am an instrument of God's love. I am an instrument of God's abundance.

I am surrounded by love. I radiate love in all directions, and love comes back to me, and it fills my soul and warms my spirit.

I am a dynamic thinker. I choose to think *only* those thoughts that serve me and serve the greater good. They contribute to my excellent health, overflowing love, and abundant prosperity. I help others create the same thing in their lives.

I picture my wonderful life! I see it, all of it, as I choose for it to be. I see it, I feel it, I enjoy it, and I know I am rich beyond my wildest dreams. I am healthy, I am fit, I am happy, I am loving, and I am loved.

I have integrity, and I am honest. I love and respect myself, and I love and respect others.

I am always safe, and I know that I am divinely protected.

I deserve the incredibly loving and special relationships that I have in my life. I deserve love. I deserve abundance. I deserve opulence. I deserve success. I deserve my wonderful friends. I deserve all the abundance of the world, and I am grateful for it all every single day.

I feel joy, and I am happy and grateful being healthy, wealthy, and loved. I am one with my ideal.

I am a powerful creator of money.

Abundance is my birthright.

I am a money magnet.

I attract money wherever I go.

My purpose and prosperity are one.

All that I need is here now.

Money is forever flowing freely in my life, and I am connected to the divine surplus.

For this and more, I am grateful. Thank you!

Index

About the Authors

Peggy McColl is the president and founder of Dynamic Destinies, Inc., an organization that trains corporate leaders, entrepreneurs, and business professionals in strategic goal setting. Her innovative work has been endorsed by some of the most renowned experts in the personal development field, including Bob Proctor, Jack Canfield, Neale Donald Walsch, Jim Rohn, Mark Victor Hansen, Caroline Myss, Gregg Braden, and Debbie Ford, among many others.

Her intensive classes, speaking engagements, goal achievement seminars, and bestselling books have inspired individuals, professional athletes, authors, and organizations to reach their maximum potential.

She is the *New York Times* bestselling author of *Your Destiny Switch*.

Brian Proctor is the vice president of business development at the Proctor Gallagher Institute, a 19-company training and development enterprise that offers seminars, programs, and one-on-one coaching to business professionals. He leads the marketing division of the company.

He is the founder of InsightOfTheDay.com.